Music
as
Medicine

❧

Deforia Lane's Life of Music, Healing, and Faith

Deforia Lane
with Rob Wilkins

ZondervanPublishingHouse
Grand Rapids, Michigan

A Division of HarperCollinsPublishers

Music as Medicine: Deforia Lane's Life of Music, Healing, and Faith
Copyright © 1994 by Deforia Lane

Requests for information should be addressed to:

🏛 ZondervanPublishingHouse
Grand Rapids, Michigan 49530

Library of Congress Cataloging-in-Publication Data

Music as medicine : Deforia Lane's life of music, healing, and faith / Deforia
Lane with Rob Wilkins.
      p.   cm.
    ISBN 0-310-20660-X
    1. Lane, Deforia, 1948–. 2. Music therapists—United States—Biography.   I.
Wilkins, Rob. II. Title
    ML429.L28A3 1995
    615.8'5154'092—dc20
    [B]   94-29129
                                                   CIP
                                                    , MN

In certain cases, the identities of individuals in this book have been masked by fictitious
names.

Edited by Linda Vanderzalm and Rachel Boers

Printed in the United States of America

97 98 99 00 01 02 / ❖ DH / 10 9 8 7 6 5 4

A beautiful autobiography of a special superstar whose music reaches into the very soul of those who are coping with cancer, a force that brings hope, joy and love and creates an awakening from suffering.

Russell F. Catanese, Executive Director
American Cancer Society, Ohio Division, Inc., Cleveland, Ohio

Deforia uses her gift of music to touch the very souls of those around her. An extraordinary book by an extraordinary woman.

Katie Skelton, RN MSN
Director of Nursing Resources,
City of Hope National Medical Center

While reading the manuscript for *Music As Medicine*, visual and verbal images of the author, Dr. Deforia Lane, appeared. I became her pastor in 1964, Phillips Temple Christian Methodist Episcopal Church, Dayton, Ohio, and had the joy of hearing her sing and seeing her mature, grow, and develop as a person of faith. Her book to me is about a person searching and struggling, and sharing the life that she searches and struggles to find.

Bishop Marshall Gilmore, Presiding Bishop
Eighth Episcopal District, the C.M.E. Church, Dallas, Texas

Deforia Lane's book tells of love, courage, and the power of music to help people in extraordinary circumstances. The story of her journey will touch the reader's heart as surely as she has touched those around her.

John Kratus, Professor of Music Education
Michigan State University

Deforia guides us through pains, fears, joys and hopes that we as humans face. This moving story will inspire others in their journey through cancer. Incredibly powerful!

Lynn Erdman, Nationally Acclaimed Speaker
Director, Presbyterian Hospital Cancer Center

Courageous, inspiring, insightful, and refreshing.... As an artist, she paints a picture for the reader of precisely how music therapy works on the people with whom she is involved. As a scientist, she describes her research into the "hows" and "whys" of music therapy. Finally, and most importantly, as a human being she bravely opens her heart and mind to the reader so that you can walk along with her during her journey.

Andrea H. Farbman, Ed. D., Executive Director
National Association for Music Therapy
Silver Spring, MD

I dedicate this book in memory of my dear father,
Mr. Elbert Sims,
who nurtured me richly with his love,
anchored me in his discipline,
and faithfully provided a home
of enduring security for all the members of his family.
I also dedicate this to a woman
who epitomizes the Christian woman;
one who has a heart to serve others,
who loves me unconditionally,
and has graced my world with music—
my mother, my friend, my inspiration,
Mrs. Gloria Sims.

Contents

Acknowledgments

I owe my deepest gratitude to Rob Wilkins for his incomparable gift of writing and his sensitive Christian spirit. He captured my life and the lives of my parents with depth, integrity, and wisdom beyond his years.

Thank you also to:

my husband, Ernest Luther Lane, whose love and support gave me the confidence and freedom to tell my story as the Lord prompted;

my mother, Gloria Sims, who kept me focused when I was tempted to let up, who prayed, counseled, and prayed some more;

my sister, Deborah McLoud, who beautifully relived and retrieved a host of memories from our childhood that I had long forgotten;

my brother, Howard Sims, who listened to me and assured me as I wrestled with doubts about what to include and what to omit;

my son, Martin Lane, who believes in his mom and told me so when I most needed to hear it;

my son, Curtis Lane, who has kept me laughing and tuned in to life's humorous side;

my mother-in-law, Mrs. Irma Lane, who raised a son with such loving care that he is the best husband and father the world has ever known;

my friends, Ron and Gloria Jackson and Kathy Harmon, who always told me that I should "write a book";

and, above all, my humble thanks to my Lord and Savior Jesus Christ, who allowed me the privilege of sharing the life he has given me through this book.

Part One

The Movements
of Grace

Since I am coming to that holy room
Where with thy choir of saints for evermore,
I shall be made thy music, as I come
I tune the instrument here at the door,
And what I must do then, think here before.

John Donne, "Hymn to God, My God, in My Sickness"

*G*inny was seventeen, wrapped from head to foot in bandage, looking every bit like a mummy. The only parts of her body that remained visible were her eyes, her mouth, and three fingers on her right hand. Complications in her leukemia treatments left her with no skin. Twice a day nurses removed her bandages, scrubbed her body, and put on new bandages. Her pain, similar to that of a burn patient, was simply unimaginable. She could see only in shadows.

Before she became ill, Ginny was an active, popular, bright, and beautiful young woman, with red hair and a flair for music. She played in the orchestra. When I first met Ginny, she had been in the hospital for weeks and had become withdrawn and severely depressed. I approached her tentatively. "Ginny, I hear you were a musician in high school. I've brought an instrument with me. For you, playing it will be a piece of cake. You may play it today if you like, or I could come back another time." I wanted to give her choices, the very things that she had not had many of lately. I gently strummed the Omnichord.

Much to my surprise, Ginny said, "I'll play now." For the next forty-five minutes, she sang and played her heart out. I remember singing "That's What Friends Are For."

> Keep shining, keep smiling,
> Knowing you can always count on me;
> For sure, Ginny, that's what friends are for;
> In good times, in bad times,
> I'll be on your side forevermore;
> That's what friends are for.

As Ginny played with those three unbandaged fingers, her mother and aunt cried. When I left, I told Ginny to jot down the names of some songs that she would like to play during my next visit. Ginny chuckled. As her mother escorted me to the door, I heard Ginny say, "Auntie, get the notepad, I've thought of a song." Her mother told me it was the first time Ginny had smiled since she had been in the hospital. That was a Friday. Over the weekend, Ginny died. For her memorial service, at her mother's request, I sang: "Keep shining, keep smiling . . . I'll be on your side forevermore."

Chapter One

An Arrangement of Grace

Da Capo (from the beginning)

In the activity room of Rainbow Babies and Children's Hospital, surrounded by the painted and crayoned flowers, whales, and houses, is the beginning of an agenda. For me, the music therapist, it is the unfolding of another day, a census on floor two.

Alyson Grossman—the child-life specialist—student volunteers, and I have our checklists: rooms, names, conditions, contributing factors, special needs. We are professional, crisp, and often given to humor, as we must be in the never-ending weight of such words. "The fourteen-year-old boy in bed 13 in the ICU has a sinus infection that got so bad, they had to resect part of his brain," Alyson begins. "He opens his eyes, but we haven't seen anything purposeful. It doesn't look good for the long term. His parents are distraught."

I note the facts.

"Bed 1: Omar Harris, oncology, sixteen years old, brain tumor, 2 West. He's been here since November, when he had a bone-marrow transplant. He is a pleasant boy; his mom stays overnight with him. We're going to celebrate his birthday tomorrow; it was Friday, but he just didn't feel up to celebrating then."

That reminds me of something. "Have you heard anything from Chandra?" I ask. "I was looking at my rolodex the other day, saw her address, and I realized I haven't talked to her since she left." They say they haven't heard from her. We all feel the weight of trying to stay connected with too many people.

"Bed 2: Misty, age fourteen, cerebral palsy with respiratory problems. Intubated and on dialysis three times a week, arms contorted, contracted. She is not spastic. We are making plans to begin transferring her now. Her parents, who are very faithful, are looking for a nursing home. Misty seemed very sad for about a week but now is very alert, responsive."

I note these facts, as well as details about other patients. Then Alyson continues. She has a list of those who may be down for my music-therapy group session: Tiara, four years old, with cerebral palsy and a cast; Brittany, eighteen months old, a tibia fracture; Walter, three years old, swallowed a coin; Alex, sixteen months, cranial reconstruction; and so on.

After she finishes her list, I laugh. This will be a challenge: a wide variety of ages and problems. "I don't know why I'm acting as if you're to blame for this potpourri of kids," I say. I know by now not to expect any kind of order in this chaos. We have to be prepared for anything.

"Anyone else?" I ask. "Others I could visit?" I make further notes: Gina, twelve, third floor, just had her leg amputated at the knee; Crystal, twelve years old, spinal fusion with a halo cast; Nicole, room 23, age six, has myelodysplasia, had a seizure.

That's it. That's enough. At 10:11 A.M. the meeting ends and my work begins.

Life in death, the strange and powerful coupling of joy and sorrow, the fierce and tender reach of the human spirit, untouchable things like music, longing, love, and fear. I have tried to come to grips with such things; yet, I know of no language that can express what I have experienced and what I have yet to learn.

How can words begin to tell of life? Of the wonderful, awkward, moving, horrible, and overwhelming things? Of my cold cries of despair? Of the warm laughter of God? Of the mystery in struggle and the wildness in joy? I am moved, more times than not, to metaphor: *like* and *as*, the telling of a story, the flow and cut of poetry.

For it is metaphor, by definition and design, that connects. Through *like* and *as*, words bring ideas together. Through the telling of a story, we see through other people's eyes. What is important is what touches and maybe somehow changes the thoughts and lives of others.

I am by profession a music therapist. Technically, music therapy is the systematic application of music to aid in the treatment of the physiological or psychological aspects of an illness or disability. Off the record, it is much more magical than that: music and healing are often matters of the human spirit. Because of the nature of my job, I have witnessed more than a few miracles, miracles worth telling and retelling.

Yet in some ways, I am embarrassed to tell *my* story. Who am I to be asked to write an autobiography? What have I really done to merit such attention? The answers, quite honestly and quite refreshingly, are *absolutely no one* and *absolutely nothing*. Yet I am a child of the living God, bearing his image, doing his works. I no longer wrestle with such paradox. It is enough for me to know this: through bouts with insecurity and pride, health and sickness, I have learned that every good and perfect thing comes from above. It comes as a gift, a gift of grace. Grace is the strange poetry of God and humans, the holy and the stained, the unmerited flow of the divine through sin-choked hearts. Each of us has been wonderfully and inexplicably gifted to serve God, to be like him.

God has chosen to work through me in some unique ways through his marvelous and transcendent gift of music. He has allowed me to interact at the level of soul with the wounded and hungry image of God, with the human capacity for destruction or holiness, despair or faith.

I have seen the impossible, the unimaginable: a woman brought out of a coma by a song; a mother tenderly bathing the gray-green skin of her dead five-year-old son; a mentally retarded and mute child who learned to sing; and my own life, gripped by fear and disease, restored.

But all of these things were not the result of my own efforts. I merely experienced God's working through me and through others. My work has been simply this: to believe in the Son of God. To believe, against all odds, that he can work through me. And that, in this broken world, is no small task.

When I find fourteen-year-old Misty in the pediatric ICU, she is wearing clown pajamas and blue earrings. Her teddy bear cuddles her face. Cerebral palsy has contorted her arms and hands until they are gnarly and claw-like; one arm is in a cast. The machines surrounding her grind and buzz and beep, the steady and steel-like chatter of the facts.

The room vibrates with contrasts: the red and green inflatable ornaments, the 700 Club on the nine-inch television, something about the mystery of the Incarnation, the way the bow has been tied in Misty's hair with precision and care, the fatigued and loving touch of Misty's mother. Just thirty pounds of humanity and the weighty machines: tubes, wires, Servo Ventilator, 900C, 12.0; Volumetric Infusion Pump; Dopamine 1 meg/kg, the red alarming numbers of a monitor—97, 116, 94, 108, 112, 97, fluctuations of a moment, the measurement of a heart. The charts are blue and yellow, on purpose, not to flash pressure, the black-and-whites of the diagnosis, treatment, prognosis. The sign in the window of Misty's room warns: PLEASE REFRAIN FROM DISCUSSING MY CONDITION OR OTHER PATIENTS' CONDITIONS OVER MY BED. I CAN UNDERSTAND. Misty, I am sure, would like to speak her feelings in words, but she can't. Never has been able to. But she understands when all is not well.

As I walk toward Misty, I hear a nurse just outside the room: "Send for blood for David, one unit of FFT, stat." I wonder how music will fly in the midst of this necessary chaos. I wonder how it will reach through the precision and the urgency of metal and voice, and touch.

"Misty," I say and introduce myself. "Rose told me that you and Ginny had a great time playing with my instrument yesterday. I heard your favorite song is 'Sesame Street.'" Misty softly stares at me, searching my eyes. "I thought you might like to play again. Blink once if you want me to play. Blink twice if you want me to take a hike." Misty wants the music.

"Can you tell me how to get to Sesame Street?" I sing and Misty plays the Omnichord, an oval-shaped, touch-sensitive synthesizer, which can be strummed with a finger or even a toe. Misty plays with her unbroken, contorted hand. "Can you tell me how to get to Sesame Street?" I keep my eyes with hers. "Beautiful, Misty. You strum just right."

We begin again, another song. Amidst the gauges and monitors and charts—12.2, 106, 900 C, 30 lbs, 14 yrs., 1 meg, saline and psychotropic—we do a song:

I see a girl named Misty.
Oh, I met a girl named Misty.
Hello,
Hello.

Just outside the room, chaos reigns. The jangle of voices, phones, orders mix with the cries of a two-year-old in pain.

I see a girl named Misty.
Oh, I met a girl named Misty.
Hello,
Hello.

As the song ends, I see the hint of a smile, something that moved somewhere behind her eyes. I lean down and say, "You have the most beautiful eyes, Misty. My goodness, I wish I had lashes that long."

In a moment, Misty shuts those beautiful eyes. She is tired. She sleeps, in bed 2 of the pediatric ICU, the soft browns in the red alarms, for a moment or two, floating on a dream or a song.

I check my notes, orient myself: Gina, twelve years old, leg amputated because of recurrent cancer, third floor. I maneuver my cart of musical instruments, a multicolored parachute, and streamers onto the elevator and out onto the floor, the overflow of sick children. "Gina? Two doors down on the left," the nurse indicates. I stand there, outside the door of another patient with a grave illness. Me, with my song and dance. In these moments I feel like a helpless stranger.

Gina, with her gold wire-rim glasses and short blond-brown hair, sits in her bed. The hint of a smile tugs at the corners of her lips, deeper creases, in one so young, of despair. She cradles a worn-out teddy bear and giggles whenever she can. I can barely introduce myself: I see her wrestling down her words, sputtering in her energy, waiting as patiently as she can for me to hurry up and finish.

"I love music," she finally is able to say, stringing her words together more in a child's excitement than an adult's sense of logic. "I play the French horn in junior high, and take singing lessons, and I've only had about ten lessons so far, and I learned how to breathe, how to position myself, that kind of stuff. I used to play the piano, took lessons from first through sixth grade, but I had to quit it because of the stress and all. There were times, in between the hospitals, that I wanted to scream whenever I sat down to play. I love singing, though, and my teacher is really neat, and I think I would like to be a singer."

I wait for her to pause for a breath, which she finally does.

"I think we're going to get along very well," I say to her. She smiles. I feel it all the way down in my toes.

With a fresh breath, she is wound up again: "Have you ever played a French horn before?"

"No," I say. "How does that work? I always wondered how they got so much music out of those three little keys." On the third floor of a hospital, a child explains the workings of a French horn, with her voice dancing, in music, in the ring of her laugh.

There is color here, not only in Gina's voice, but also in what surrounds her: cards, balloons, a fruit basket, flowers, all in the primary and vital energy of a child—reds, yellows, oranges, bright blues, with overpowering splashes of will, the turning back of the black-and-white progress of a black-and-white disease. She wants to be a singer.

There are dreams here, beyond Gina's flowing French horn theory, solid dreams: a picture of Hawaii on the wall, the beauty of rock and water, and her mother sitting, as she has done so many times before, by her daughter's hospital bed. The cancer, I know, has taken something from her too. It has changed the definition of her smile, maybe; but never, not even once, has it touched the laughter in her eyes when she sees her child move on in chatterbox rhythm to the music of her dreams.

I never fail to be humbled by such strength.

The bed next to Gina is occupied by a girl in her late teens. The girl's mother and another visitor join us. Everyone wants to play some music. I reach for my tone chimes, which are similar to tuning forks with rubber knockers. "Cool," Gina says. "It sounds like a doorbell." As I distribute an instrument to each person in the room, I hear fits of giggles.

In the background is the sound of the television, "ABC News," a story about a Missouri man who loves wild horses.

"What's your favorite song?" I ask Gina.

"Umm, I don't know. That's a hard one."

"Wild and content," the man on the television says, "for the time being."

"Do you know 'Lean on Me'?" I ask.

19

Gina nods.

Following my instructions for each person to wait on his or her cue, we begin. We all sing.

Sometime in our lives, (cue Gina)
We all have pain, (cue Gina's roommate)
And we all have sorrow. (cue Gina's mom)
But if we are wise, (another cue)
We know that there's always tomorrow.

There is laughter in the teaming of notes, the pushing back of monotony and fear, the common thread of music. The television is almost forgotten, the man about horses: graceful and free, with no fences. When the song ends, we applaud each other, a break in the walls of disappointment, routine, and pain.

"I love to hear you sing," I say to Gina.

"Sometimes after surgery," she says, "I don't sing too good; there's stuff in my throat. It's hard to learn to position yourself to sing like a diva," she adds, referring to her voice lessons, "when you spend so much time on your back."

We sing another song, using different instruments this time. We share more laughter.

The television story drones in the background. The man with the wild horses speaks of the danger of losing freedom.

When we finish, I ask Gina if she might like to try to write a song. I would help. "You appear to me to be bright, very creative, that's obvious."

She has to be she says. There's so much stuff to slow her down, fences that impede her freedom. When the pain had first started in her leg, it was so bad that she missed school; the doctor told her it was tendonitis.

"You're feisty, too, I see. We're going to get along just famously."

"If I wrote a song, that would be some song," she says. "People would start to cry." I tell her that sometimes when you say something sad or sing something sad it makes you feel better. "I have cancer," she says without a hint of anger, as a matter of fact. "I've had it twice, and that's not something I usually share with people."

"Have you ever written any poetry?" I ask.

The television story continues: the horses are penned in, no longer free to move at will.

"Once," she giggles, "when I was little. I didn't tell anybody about it, 'cause it was so stupid." Without any cue, she recites the lines she can remember.

> In summer days,
> I like to run and play.

Underneath her sheets, Gina shuffles, as if to remind herself of what is missing, and smiles. "That was the first poem I ever wrote." I ask her if I could come back and visit her some time. She says she would love it. She has this thing for music. She wants to be a singer.

The man on television says that if something is not done, we'll all be less free.

My life, when I have tried to break it down into meaningful pieces, has often become a puzzle. When I begin to look at *this* event or *that* circumstance or *those* years, the focus moves from the whole to the parts. I no longer see the thread that holds it all together, and things begin to unravel in fear, doubt, or addiction.

I have come to view my life as the score of a song that is composed of movements: andante, allegro, rondo. . . . At times, each line seems carefully constructed, a movement of purpose and rhythm. In the expected changes of tempo, grand entrances and exits, points of dissonance and climax, I am tempted to relax. At other times, the lines seem cacophonous, thin, lacking structure, form, or focus. In the perceived chaos, I am given to panic.

Yet I have learned that while each movement is separate and distinct, with its own texture, tone, and rhythm, together they flow in a continuity of design and purpose. Like music, life

21

has its own momentum, a pull from beyond ourselves: through our mistakes, attached to our longing, aching or bursting in transition, expecting a climax. Like music, life is composed of the movement of change, often laced with recurrent themes and repetitious pain, but seeking nonetheless a determined sort of beauty, soul, grace, and newness.

Like music, life depends on the quality of the composition. The music of Bach is different from the music played on MTV.

For Christians, the composer of life is none other than Yahweh himself, the great, creative, powerful, one and only God of the cosmos. Life, birthed in the very image of God, is designed to be purposeful, dynamic, pulsing with holy momentum. In the same way a river empties itself into the sea, the song of creation flows toward a center that always holds its own.

The music, I have come to believe, is nothing less than a soul at praise.

I have, on a rare occasion, experienced such purity of line—worship, song, touch of God—when time stops, swallowed by the eternal, caught up in the rushing wind of Spirit: the lingering note of an aria launched in longing, a frightened and hopeful touch of a hand, the angle of a psalm. And I have wondered: Why are such moments so fleeting, so rare, so covered with pain and day-to-day realities?

The moments pass, one by one. From room to room, I walk the halls, my rounds of another working day. In the still-wet paint of the time recently past I see the wild and subtle brush strokes of an artist, a fanatic, or a child. Maybe a little of each. Who could guess at such a world: where a sunset births such a fecundity of color, a virtual screaming of pastels; where a mother strolls with her six-month-old son, his head wrapped like a mummy, and listens to him coo contentedly? A world of endless surprise.

I stop to see Crystal in 228, her father with a newspaper, her mother holding her hand, her big sister in charge of crayons. Crystal has a spinal fusion with a "halo," a metal half-hoop screwed into her skull to keep her head from moving. "If she spits up any more blood," the doctor was saying as I arrive, "let me know."

Crystal, when you first meet her, has the shy smile of a ten-year-old. She isn't sure if she wants to play music, but she warms up when she gets to name the musical instruments in Spanish so that her mother can understand. Then, before we sing and play, she tells me who gets what: big sister, maraca; mom, cabasa. She reserves the clatterpillar, a sort of wooden slinky, for herself. The music brings Crystal out of herself, makes her forget about her halo and her IV pricks. We sing to the accompaniment of her family's band: "Angelos milando a mi, tota El Dio. . . ." All day, all night, angels watching over me, my Lord. Angels watching over me. For a short time, we laugh and make music. Then as I prepare to leave, she is aware again of her halo. Angelos milando a mi. . . .

In the afternoon I meet with Dean, a forty-year-old man with Down's syndrome. When I arrive, he is watching "Gomer Pyle" as Bobo, his bear, looks on. His sister, almost always at his side, has gone somewhere, and he looks lonely. "Do you want to play some music, Dean?" He clears his throat, unable to speak many words intelligibly, and signs a yes. On the Omnichord, we play "You Are My Sunshine," and Dean, with great effort, strums up and down.

"Yesterday, you did 'Jesus Loves Me' so well. Would you like to do that again, Dean?" No response. "Dean, would you like to do 'Jesus Loves Me' again?" Again he signs a yes. With Dean strumming and me singing, we move through the song. "Dean, would you like to sing with me, this time?" We begin the song again. I place Dean's hand on my throat when I sing "me" and then put his hand on his throat.

After several attempts, hand to my throat, hand to his throat, Dean finally sings, in a whisper, "Me."

"Yes," I said, and then resumed, "Yes, Jesus loves me; Yes, Jesus loves . . ."

"Me," came another soft whisper.

23

Sin, and its consequent fallout of evil, involves decomposition. It seeks to destroy all that God in his perfect love has composed. "The wages of sin is death," the apostle writes, the evening news proves. The music in life—the sound the soul should make in movement to God—is often distorted and warped. Disconnected from its source, the song is trapped in self, the endless echo of what it means to be alone in a treacherous world. Survival is often the name of that tune. What remains is the noise of getting by: sirens, demands, screams, gunfire.

I hear it all the time. With many of the patients I see at the hospital, it's hard to tell where the sin ends and the disease begins. Broken bones, broken relationships. Babies with AIDS, babies with addictions. Babies with bruises, parents with no sense of regret. Cancer and smoke, strokes and anger, heart attacks and stress, infection and promiscuity, aneurysms and obesity. With each one of us claiming the title of "victim," what is left for the truly innocent?

I should talk. Watch if I sing the blues too. When it comes to my own sin, I am amazed at my ability to flash between ignorance and despair. Neither is appropriate, but such extremes seem much easier than dealing with the pain and damage, than facing the music I have decomposed.

I say this because I want to be honest. Some sin in my life has settled so deeply that I wonder if the music I know is merely the drumming of my own head. How is it possible in a world and heart prone to sin to sing with purity and selflessness?

The answer is only this: by grace. For in God—the love of the Father, the redemption of the Son, the guidance of the Spirit—is not only the composition of life but also an ongoing and creative arrangement of grace.

A theory in music states that once a sound is created, it becomes eternal. If that is true, we can no sooner stop a song than we can drink the Atlantic Ocean. I have learned that grace is like the pulse and flow in a song. When we are longing for

God, and sometimes when we are not, grace breaks through—arranging the composition, scoring the soul, empowering the gifts—and draws us inexorably to the masterful embrace of the Great Composer.

At the end of the day I see David, a black man in his mid-thirties. He plays the saxophone in a band. When I walk in his room, he is at the Yamaha keyboard I had lent him. He tells me he played music until five o'clock in the morning. No wonder he looks bleary-eyed.

David creates music. "I sorta make it up as I go along, and then all of a sudden, I get caught up in something." Although he has never taken lessons on a keyboard, he picks it up quickly. The music moves through him. "Blues, jazz, gospel, jam, R & B. I'm all around," he says.

David has been in the hospital for over a month now. He had a kidney transplant, but something is not draining. The doctors have inserted a catheter and are waiting. David has hopes of going home soon. When I ask him how he is doing, he plays a few notes, the blues, and sings "Stuck some kind of stem in me." More blue notes, "Come back for an operation on Monday." More of the blues, "Don't look like anything is going to happen right away." Yet David has learned to roll with the punches. In music, the kind that keeps him up until five o'clock in the morning, he has learned to find the rest he needs.

Life's song doesn't belong to any one of us; it's not a possession like an Oldsmobile or a 1928 buffalo nickel. We must not be fooled into believing that we can pawn it or hoard it or stash it in a Swiss bank account. The song must be a shared experience.

It's easy for me to see the people who pass through my life as fellow musicians, singers. Each person adds to the song a different interpretation, tempo, mood, and lyric; every human intersection adds a different crescendo, diminuendo, or forte. The part that each of us plays influences the quality of the song.

The church, God's community, is like an orchestra. In this community are different instruments—woodwinds, percussion, strings—and different parts—leads, harmonies, counter melodies. Not everyone plays the same note at the same time or with the same accent. Sometimes one instrument plays the melody while others play supportive, seemingly monotonous undertones. But each role, whether the melody of the violin or the repetition of a tuba, is critical to the formation of the chord. Individual efforts flow into one another. The music is more than a reflection of the community; it is its offspring.

Such community, of course, requires hard work: years of practice, lessons, failure, and discipline. Harmony of community does not simply happen by accident. Each member must learn how to compensate for others' failures, to cover their mistakes, to forgive their glitches. It is a discipline to live in an imperfect world made up of imperfect people.

The community shares a vision: the art of beauty, the connection with one another, the loosing of the very voice of God. When a gifted and disciplined community is obedient to a higher call, anything can happen. The product, the art, is of far greater value than the sum of the parts. Members of an orchestra say that at times, beyond the limitations of space and time and human capability, the music simply takes over. The musicians are no longer the players; they *become* the instruments themselves, conduits for something beyond them.

So it should be with the community of God. Each person—gifted, disciplined, obedient, forgiving—is collectively birthed in a symphony of grace, a community of life, at one with beauty.

*L*orrie was twenty-one, developmentally delayed, and had the mentality of a twelve-year-old. She had had her eye surgically removed after cancer had spread to it, and wore an eye patch. I was taken with Lorrie from the beginning, not just for the strength with which she faced her challenges, but with the simplicity and fortitude of her faith.

Her favorite song was "Jesus Loves Me," and although she did not have a particularly good singing voice, she would often take my breath away when she sang it. There was something about the simplicity of the message, the sincerity with which she sang, the girl who had little to cling to except the truth in those words.

As I worked with Lorrie, she asked if I would help her compose another verse of "Jesus Loves Me." After much work, she wrote:

> Jesus died on Calvary's tree;
> He's done so many things for me;
> He helped me walk and he made me whole;
> Oh, what a miracle, he saved my soul.

Lorrie's cancer progressed, finally leaving her in a coma. One day as I sat over her, I sang "Jesus Loves Me," including the verse she had written, and then asked her, "Isn't that beautiful, Lorrie?" Incredibly, Lorrie nodded her head yes. For a short while, she recovered and returned home. I visited her, and when Lorrie would become agitated her mother would calm her with the words of "Jesus Loves Me." Eventually, Lorrie's cancer overtook her and she died. I often wondered if, as Lorrie went to her Creator, nestled child-like in the arms of her Father, those simple and innocent words were on her mind.

Chapter Two

Childhood: Dancing in 0/0 Time

Dolce (softly, sweetly)

My mother's music, the intimacy of one soul and one piano, always stopped us in our tracks. Her music was to us children like the smell of popcorn: penetrating, inviting, and unavoidable. My sister, Deborah, and I could have been anywhere, in any number of fantasy kingdoms, and our imaginations would have been no match to the reality of the music. We were drawn to it.

Sometimes we would just listen. My mom preferred the romantic, expressive pieces—the swirling, eddying crescendos and pianissimos of Debussy or Chopin—rather than the precise, studied order and repetition of Bach or Mozart. She was a forever romantic, private at her piano.

Other times our mother would rip into a slightly more infectious number, say "Humoresque," "Scarf Dance," or "Polonaise," and we, with the souls of children, couldn't help dancing. Some songs, lodged in certain timeless moments, made us move. So there we were, my sister and I, maybe seven and five, even then so different in style and composition, moving hand in hand bad-ballet-style, arms and legs flailing in pirouette and arabesque, touched by the music. We would circle faster and faster, caught in the force and the music, giggling up and down a crescendo, finally falling on our faces, exhausted.

Moments of dancing, lost in laughter and music, are both fleeting and eternal. When I look back on my childhood, I generally do not recall details like dates or events. I attribute this not only to poor memory but also to the nature of childhood. In the rising of consciousness, children are only vaguely aware of the passing of time, in much the same way a skier is aware of snow. Children, unlike so many adults, do not try to slice time into definable units but simply go with the flow. The song of childhood is played in 0/0 time.

What I remember of my childhood are mostly moments and faces, which do not stick to any well-defined logic or linear history: fireflies at twilight, the ice cream stand on Sunday, the large and gentle hands of my father, the ambulance at the house next door.

Who knows the sequence in which these moments played themselves out? Why should a child concern herself with space, time, and order? Imagination and need rule the child's world and give root to almost all childhood memories. What sticks in the mind is the freedom of play and the discipline of love. Childhood is, more than any other time of our lives, all about *experiencing* life, not trying to control it with months, days, hours, minutes, and seconds. In childhood, anything is likely to happen, precisely because anything *can* happen.

The freshness of experience makes for a world of wonder, wildness, and imagination. The child stores such experience of sensation, emotion, and the ever-present Now. That is why I have such a difficult time recalling childhood, much less putting it into words on paper. For better or worse, I now think almost entirely as an adult—in a logical sequence anchored heavily to time—and as a consequence I have often lost that uniquely childlike quality of surprise. I struggle with whatever I cannot order. Therefore childhood in hindsight usually looks like a series of wildly unconnected and dynamic events.

Among the bits and pieces, I recall a general mood, a remnant of childhood. In most cases, we don't look back on childhood with neutrality. The experience is usually overwhelmingly positive or negative. Living life attuned to wonder, wildness, and imagination is risky business. Without an environment of love, a child's world can turn dangerous at the drop of a hat. A child, in a world of cool hearts, may cease to take chances, seeking love in numbness, disconnected thrill, or rage. A child always fears going unnoticed.

My childhood was blessed. I'm not talking about possessions, for by many people's standards we were poor, growing up in a lower-middle-class area of Dayton, Ohio. I was rich in love and safety. I suppose that you could argue that these were my *possessions* as a child, but they did not depend on my ownership and nurture for their existence; in fact, they often wilted when I sought to hold them too tightly. The love and safety I felt were the gifts of loving parents. They came from an arrangement of grace.

Such grace was the stuff of hard work, discipline, and perseverance. As a child, my father farmed and worked Louisiana cotton fields. My mother was the daughter of a carpenter. Living as blacks in the segregated South, they learned the unnatural and oppressive order of things. *Nigger* was a word they lived with, and opportunity was slow to knock.

My parents made decisions early on in their lives about what to do with the anger, the shape that injustice took in their hearts. First, they learned how to survive. They knew what to say and what not to say, what to do and what not to do. They played the game of "keeping in their places." Through their submission, I believe, they created opportunities to free themselves, or at least their children. They chose not to nurture anger, not to burn their souls on bitterness. They refused to return hate for hate. If it had to come to a choice, they preferred to allow themselves to be abused rather than become one of the abusers. The energy that many blacks consumed in anger, my parents channeled into fortitude.

My parents both moved from the South to the Dayton area in the 1940s. My mother, Gloria, one of the few blacks of the time with the benefit of a college education, moved in with her sister's family. My father, Elbert Sims, who was not afforded the opportunity for formal education, found work at the General Motors plant and moved in with family friends.

My parents met at a company picnic and shared a sandwich and a lifetime of values. Both were deeply entrenched in the work ethic. They determined the future could and would be brighter. But, unlike so many workers in today's culture, they were not dreaming in a vacuum. Their hard work was tied to values, a strong sense of right and wrong and a desire to give and not just get. Even before they were married, my parents had determined to give of themselves to their children.

After their wedding in 1947, my parents moved into the upstairs room in my aunt's home. I was their first child. I have a black-and-white picture of my father and mother and their newborn, Deforia. My father is in suit and tie, neatly pressed and dapper, the orderly carryover of his military service. My mother is in a black dress, white earrings, and white sash. She is smiling. Dwarfed by a huge but gentle hand, I am cradled in my father's left arm. My father stands with head tilted slightly back, one eyebrow raised, eyes caught in a blink, a camera's view of a proud man in love. I was asleep, safe. If the picture said nothing else, it spoke of the promise that they would provide for me.

My father worked thirty years for General Motors as a crane operator, appliance sprayer, and production worker. Once the company offered him a promotion with the provision that he pass a math test. Because my father spent his childhood working to support his family, he had not had a chance to learn formal math. Although my daddy was a wise man, his intelligence fell outside the pencil-and-paper math test. He did not pass the test and did not get the promotion. That was the only time I sensed my father's disappointment in himself; it came at about the same time his arthritis began to cripple him in the knees.

My mother worked as a data processor at the Wright Patterson Air Force Base. She once turned down a promotion that would have spiraled her into the world of management. She knew that it would cost her resources she needed for her family. My mother has always had an instinct for what is needed. Over a period of twenty-five years, she worked as an IBM operator, computer clerk, supervisor, mother, wife, and homemaker.

Together, each working a different shift, my parents provided a present and a future for their three children. My sister, Deborah, was born two years after my birth, and my brother, Howard, was born eight years after Deborah. Our parents were both frugal. My father knew how to stretch one pound of beef over three days of meals, and my mother wore the same thrift-shop dresses for decades, looking always beautiful. They saved enough money to build a house when I started high school as well as to provide a college education for their children.

But that was the least of what they provided. Most importantly they gave us love, an unshakable sense of security. My father towers in my memory. Strong, tall, handsome, and proud, he loved to get down on the floor and tickle us. I remember him lying on his back and giving us each a ride on his feet. We exhausted him, always shouting for more, never satiated with this attention.

What I most remember of my father comes through special moments or routines: the Sunday drives in the green Buick on a late spring day; the rare and unexpected stop at the corner ice cream store; the early morning fishing trips, a sunrise low and rose on the water, the same color of my father's laughter as I beat my slimy fish off the hook. I can still hear his baritone voice, always above the rest in church, singing "Precious Lord, Take My Hand" or prodding me, "Girl, get your lessons."

The whole family depended on my father as our ever-present chauffeur, since Mom did not drive when we were young. He invested many miles and much time in seeing to it that his wife and children got to choir rehearsals, piano lessons, youth council meetings, recitals, afternoon church teas, Bible studies, and church programs. We must have driven him crazy, but still he continued.

My father, like his father before him, was a strict disciplinarian. He tolerated no sass. He demanded respect. We chil-

33

dren knew what was expected of us, and if we disobeyed, he punished us with switches, leather belts, or his huge hands. Because I was often headstrong, I remember some of those spankings.

My love for my father was sometimes mixed with fear. He looms so large in my childhood because of the awkward tension of wanting to please him one moment and to avoid his discipline the next. He could strike the fear of God in me. I remember one time when I was about ten, my father had cooked black-eyed peas. I had convinced myself that I hated black-eyed peas. My father said either to eat the peas or to just sit there. At ten o'clock I was still sitting at the table, and my father went to bed. When I thought he was asleep, I left my peas and fixed myself a peanut butter and Argo syrup sandwich. Just as I was about to take my first bite, I heard his footsteps coming down the stairs. I panicked, opened the basement door, and threw my sandwich into a corner. I returned to my chair, guilt smeared across my face. "Hi, Daddy," I said, as he entered the kitchen and walked past me.

"I see those black-eyed peas are still there," he said, walking toward the basement door.

"Uh-huh," I returned meekly.

He opened the door, found the sandwich, and looked at me. I can still see the look on his face; I can still feel the fear that look instilled. Within minutes, I had eaten every black-eyed pea on my plate.

As much as my father loved me and I loved him, there was sometimes a certain distance between us. Part of the distance, most of it probably, existed in my mind. I tried not only to avoid his discipline but also to earn his praise. I felt compelled to do something to make him proud. I wanted to feel safe, away from his discipline and anchored in his love.

In looking back, I see my father's distance as self-protective. He was introspective, a thinker, deep and knowing. Especially as he got older, he would escape into an inner refuge, a private place somewhere behind his eyes. He was still loving, but bent in his knees and in his dreams for himself. He was both the child of hard times and the father of my potential.

But for me as a child, Daddy was always a pillar of strength—the one with my world in his hands. I caught occasional glimpses of his vulnerability, his dependency. One picture in particular, reinforced many times over the years, was the sight of my father in prayer. On his arthritic knees, beside his bed, head bowed, forehead cradled in his large hands, he would pray to his Father. The sight would almost always shake me; he looked so vulnerable and humble, almost like a child himself. This was my father, whom I knew as the all-powerful one.

Sometimes he would pray for a long time, pouring out his heart inaudibly, confidentially, consistently. I remember often wondering what Daddy talked to God about and why he took so long. What secret dreams, hopes, and confessions echoed toward heaven? And what did God say back to him? Once I even asked my daddy what he said when he prayed. He told me that he was thanking God, expressing a heart of gratitude and thankfulness, never wanting to forget where he had come from and how God had pulled him through. As a child, I didn't know much about this side of my father; I think I instinctively knew that too much of such a sight would strip me of the sense of security and refuge that my father provided. I simply would not have possessed the maturity to understand.

I did not often see Daddy as tender; he was not always easy to please. He worked hard to instill discipline and a sense of morality in his children. Nothing could be done sloppily. Commitments were to be kept. Practice was essential. Homework was to be finished. A swear word, even a "darn," was unacceptable.

Deborah, Howard, and I were the pride of our daddy's life. In our hearts we knew that. Yet he would seldom praise us directly. I would overhear him talking on the phone about an award I had received. Or we would stop over at our relatives on the way home from fishing so that they could see a string full of bluegills we had caught. I was often left to interpret a nod of the head, a hint of a smile, or a hand on the shoulder as mean-

35

ing that Daddy was proud of me. The love and pride in my father were so deep that they sometimes failed to surface in a direct expression.

My mother was softer, more given to art than command, shaping with her presence. When I look back on my childhood, I remember my mother not specifically in special moments but with an undefined sense of her being everywhere, in every moment. She just seemed always to be there. I was, and still am, a talker. Perhaps her greatest gift of love was her willingness to listen. She would ask me how school went, and thirty or forty minutes later she was still listening. On Saturday morning, I was allowed to get into bed with her and talk and giggle for hours. I remember how warm I felt under her blankets.

We always had the sense that my mother was carefully put together, almost self-crafted. She spoke with her appearance: hair in place, soft movement, modestly and neatly dressed, clean, feminine. My mother has always been a quiet and private person; she taught us more with the timing of her words than with their volume or quantity.

I remember my mother as creator. With a word or two, she could create an opportunity. When I would come home crying about how the other kids had made fun of my big feet, she would see it as an opportunity to show me how to redirect my anger. When I said something negative about another person, she would focus my attention on his or her good qualities. With her love for culture, my mother created a love of learning. She provided us with books, encyclopedias, crayons, music, embroidery, magazines. She purposefully shaped us with an environment. With her presence, she created a cocoon of safety. I remember when my sister and I were getting harassed by some fifth-grade boys as we walked to school; Momma would walk us to school, and without a word she would protect us.

With her music, she created something beyond words. I am one of those blessed people who cannot look back on childhood without a memory saturated in song. My mother was schooled in classical music as a child, studying with a fine black pianist, with whom she lived when she attended Spelman College.

My mother was an artist. She never *used* music, and I mean that both literally and figuratively: literally in the fact that the music was in her head; figuratively because she always played from her heart. She was a lover of music, not as a collection of notes, but as a movement of the soul. Music has both extrinsic and intrinsic worth. Music can be performed and win respect and external reward for the performer. My mother never knew music extrinsically, except for two little girls dancing themselves into a frenzy of giggles. Most people never even knew she could play the piano. Music was a hiding place of sorts for my mother, who had learned over her years of disappointment and prejudice the connection of sacrifice to love. She had learned how to protect herself and still give. While she remained guarded and often suspicious of outsiders, in the private fires of her heart, she fueled the music that flowed with longing.

In the self-absorbed world of childhood, I did not stop to consider what music meant to my mother. In looking back, I see the time my mother spent with her piano as a solace, deeply intimate. In addition to the music of Chopin and Debussy she loved the stately hymns: "Take Time to Be Holy," "Jesus Keep Me Near the Cross," "Blessed Assurance," "My Faith Looks Up to Thee." I realize now that the hymns she chose were deep with meaning, bathed in movement, and capable, for a moment or two, of transporting her to heavenly realms.

From the time I was five until I was thirteen, the heart of my childhood, I lived at 52 Bish Avenue. This was a world of my parent's creation. They supplied the love, commitment, and hard work for our home to exist in an environment of love and safety.

At first glance, 52 Bish Avenue was a two-bedroom, white shingled house with an enclosed porch. Our house was nestled in a community of older homes, solid homes of brick or stucco, homes ambushed by color and bloom, a pink-red scent that stuck on porches and in memories. From our house I could see an A & P grocery store with salt and charcoal in its windows. It was, as I look back, a proud community, making up for its lack of elegance with a determined sort of enchantment that held up to just about anything. In my child's directionless mind, I knew nothing about its sociological status: lower-middle-income neighborhood.

But it also was a world of my own imagination. Take, for example, the masonry grill in our back yard. In the eyes of an adult, it was simply a piece of stone. For me, it stood like some kind of misplaced Aztec altar, where my daddy, with zeal and sauce, religiously attended to the barbecuing. On cooler days, the wind would whip and hollow in the sinus of the grill's chimney, making music that would speak of mystery—or on days nearer Halloween, of lost souls.

Or take the basement. In a world of concrete fact, it was mostly an abandoned coal bin: an ashy kind of gray, the residue of black after a good scrubbing. From the ceiling hung a single, bare incandescent light, an eye in the darkness. A furnace stood to one side, yawning with fire, gulping air. But for us, the basement was our clubhouse, our mansion, our planet. It was where old dishtowels became curtains; boxes and crates became royal furniture; paper towels, place mats, and two giggling sisters became just about anyone we wanted—queens, fairies, princesses, or Sergeant Joe Friday. It was here that we absconded my father's and mother's old clothes and grew decades older in an afternoon. It was here that we launched a thousand up-the-stairs missions—to sneak away Grandma's shoes, to kidnap the dog, to recover a missing treasure—all without detection, all at great risk from the enemy.

During the summer, when the days got sticky with heat and boredom, the kids of my neighborhood, under my sister's direction, would bring together broken toys, trinkets, old clothes, popcorn, and cardboard boxes. It was only junk to some, maybe, but in the eyes of a child, a carnival: booths and games and prizes and crazy clothes.

Down the street, on a corner by the railroad tracks, stood a gray, tight house, shuttered and silent. To most adults, it was acceptable enough, free of trash and noise. But to the neighborhood children, it was a strange house, cramped and oppressive, the way air feels on a heavy summer day. Our bikes, the kind before gears, would seem to grind down when we passed this house, slowing seconds and speeding hearts.

And in the dusted magic of Christmas, like the snow that falls in the plastic snowman's snow-and-water globe, the season would descend on us children with such enchantment, anticipation, and wonder that we would snoop, plead, dance in our sleep, and feel so loved that we were literally beside ourselves. Christmas was the season of loving sacrifice: a two-story wooden dollhouse, a bicycle—beyond what my parents could afford, a trade-off for our crooked, teeth-at-random smiles. My world was perfect.

In a free childhood, imagination—the naming of dreams and beasts—is the wildest of all creatures, roaming in the best and worst of worlds. It creates out of nothing, attaching itself to need, and presupposing that which is only hinted at or perceived. I had an active imagination. I could at the same time imagine the best in others and the worst in me. I imagined that my successes were all deception. My childhood, free and gentle as it was, was rocked by a deep insecurity, one with which I still struggle today.

By temperament, I am vulnerable: genial, extroverted, physically awkward, caring, a born encourager. Through my environment—the love of my parents and the perceived distance of my father—I learned both the desire and need for praise. I wanted so badly to be good. I tried to please with all of my heart. I covered for friends in trouble, coveted straight As, courted discipline and obedience, carved out love with the dull knife of acceptance. I wanted, for reasons both intrinsic and extrinsic, to matter.

I was motivated by my desire to please others, often sacrificing the self-care needed to develop myself more fully. I wanted to please, but nothing was ever good enough. An A-minus could have been an A. I always felt that a friend's flaw was partially my fault.

I tended to wallow in my fault and to question rather crudely my abilities. Gym class was a "Twilight Zone." Imagine, if you will, a girl with two left feet—mammoth ones at that—sitting, sitting, continually the last pick in the eternal Kickball Game from Hell. I hated all structured and critiqued forms of kicking, throwing, running.

Boys would always throw me curveballs. Unlike my sister, whom I envied for her natural physical charm, I seldom dated in high school. I often felt graceless and decided to put my energy and talents elsewhere, in places where I could succeed.

But even my successes—the string of awards and honors—I questioned. In my secret and private fears, I believed that I would be discovered to be average, nothing special, standard. When I was in sixth grade, I remember vividly the details of an event that shattered my world. My teacher had left the room, leaving results from the IQ test on her desk. Typed on white, crisp sheets was each child's name and a number: his or her IQ score. One of the boys in the class went up and started looking over the scores, calling out names, numbers, and insults. "Becky, 98. What a moron!" Other children also went to the desk to check out the scores. I remember the tension in my muscles, the ice that spread along neurons, the frost in my heart. I dreaded the words that I knew were about to be derisively screamed by one of the boys: "Deforia, 50. What an idiot!" The teacher returned, scattering the children, before that happened.

I was dying of curiosity. Although I would never have thought of joining the other kids at the desk when the teacher was gone—that would have clearly risked seeming unpleasant to my teacher—I still wanted to know. My whole world rested on the strength of that number beside my name. In my seat, in my anxiety, I came up with a plan. I pretended to have a question that I needed to ask my teacher at her desk. As she was explaining her answer, I took sidelong glances at the test results. Hazel Kelly (my best friend, who was pretty, intelligent, everything that I wanted to be) had a 130. Smart, real smart. I continued to scan down frantically, searching for my name. When I saw the number, I died inside: 106. While the score certainly was not low, it marked what I secretly feared: I was average, run of the mill, an impostor.

My first reaction was incredulity: Am I really *that* dumb? Then came guilt: What right did I have getting As and Bs when I was really not any smarter than most of the other kids? And then came the fear that the secret would soon be out: Deforia, IQ 106, suspected to be brilliant, was not what she appeared to be.

Instead of taking solace in knowing that I made high grades from an average IQ, I simply tried harder. I had to work myself into a state of grace. And with each new accomplishment and each corresponding word of praise, I failed to notice that I was succeeding. I simply wanted more. Looking back, I realize I *was* good at what I set my mind on: pleasing others. Through discipline, perseverance, morality, and a kind spirit, I was a devoted and caring friend, an excellent student, a healer, a loving daughter, a discerner. I gave with reckless abandon. I had a gift of looking past the bad in a person to his or her potential. But the mixture of motivation—wanting to please and needing to please—was muddy, and I often failed to see my personal value.

It is not surprising that I wanted to be a healer, probably a nurse. I loved the thought of transformation: the power of a touch, a smile, a movement from not well to well.

When I was growing up, I never really gave a thought to making music a career. Although I loved music, I thought of it as somewhat frivolous, extravagant, like a marble sink. Music was nice, occasionally expressive of unknown regions, but not something I could or should make a living from.

Yet I knew, in the delicate touch of my mother's fingers, the power of music. Since I can remember, my life has always

41

been steeped in music, as much a part of my environment as oxygen and autumn. My father's baritone voice, my mother's humming while doing chores, the church choirs, Otis Redding on the family's radio, "Wings Over Jordan" on the record player: all of these were the voices of song that spoke to the deepest part of me.

I enjoyed music. When I was five, I dinged a triangle in the kindergarten choir and set in motion not just a single, serious note, but a lifetime love. I knew even then that music, especially the performing of it, would occupy a part of my life. But I never dreamed it would take center stage.

Music is more than just the notes. It always involves musicians, and I learned to love people of music. Two piano teachers and one voice coach became nurturers, feeding me music, giving me a sense for discipline, and loving me beyond my ability. I started piano when I was five, before my feet could touch the pedals. My teacher was Olga B. Gates, distinguished, cultured, proper, with a laugh that rippled like a song. Olga B. Gates was a woman of considerable girth, most of which was heart. She inspired her students with her beauty in the way she said, "Now, teacher wouldn't like that," and the way her bosom nearly suffocated you with a hug. I would get lost in her. To this day, I can still equate my love for music with my love for Olga B. Gates, who will always be huge in my life.

My second piano teacher, with whom I started lessons at age twelve, was Katherine Duncan: salt-and-pepper hair, glasses, teeth that clicked slightly, and manicured, red fingernails. She was precise and measured, with a tended fire in her music. She managed her emotions like prisoners of war, with only an occasional feeling of pride escaping from her eyes. She had green report cards that stated in bold typeface—**Piano Proficiency: Katherine Duncan Studio.** I didn't know what a studio was and I certainly didn't know a black person who had one, but I was impressed with Katherine Duncan's business-like passion.

I learned technique. I learned that music is as much a matter of the will as it is the heart. Down the side of Mrs. Duncan's green grade cards were such words as *fingering, dynamics, timing, tone,* each with a categorical judgment: *excellent, very good, good, fair, needs improvement.* Katherine Duncan was a woman of check marks, and she executed in me a drive to excel. I pushed for good grades, the check marks of her approval.

Katherine Duncan stressed the classics, with an emphasis on composition and interpretation. Once she made me learn Rachmaninoff's "Flight of the Bumble Bee," tortuously busy for a child, and then let me play a duet with her at a recital, a rare privilege that sent me soaring. Even through her measured distance, she let me know that I held a special place in her heart.

A few years into my lessons with Katherine Duncan, a strange thing began to happen. She lost her precision: my grades no longer accurately reflected where I was musically; the marks were much too generous. Slowly, the tightness and order that centered her began to unravel. When she told me that she had to stop giving lessons, she seemed out of tune. My mother told me Katherine Duncan was ill. A few months later my beloved piano teacher died of cancer.

Katherine Duncan's funeral was the first one that meant anything to me. Maybe it was the way she looked in the casket or maybe it was my parents' reaction, but something about that funeral reassured me, checked my sadness with hope, and measured, for the first time in my life, the idea of eternity. Mrs. Duncan's husband, knowing of Katherine's fondness for me, invited me to come to their house and pick out of her belongings anything that I wanted. I left her home with pictures of musicians, music books, jewelry boxes: the neatly stacked legacy of my love and respect for Katherine Duncan.

A third teacher who influenced me was Josephine Stevenson, my voice teacher. We found her by referral, a hundred miles it seemed in the country. Mrs. Stevenson was strong, with jet-black hair, slightly skewed teeth, and a straightforward style. She was wonderful with me, always blooming in personality, and largely responsible for the direction in my musical life. We worked on arias, mostly in foreign languages, and English art songs—Purcell, Handel, those composers who could arrange the best repertoire for a promising young soprano. Mrs. Stevenson was serious about my talent and committed herself to direct my abilities in much the same way that an accomplished conductor leads an orchestra.

Mrs. Stevenson provided a direction to the often random movement in my life. She conditioned me for the music that best suited my voice, diction, and stage presence. She enlisted me in competitions where awards began to confirm in my mind her opinion of my musical ability. Finally, when I was a senior in high school and after two years of voice lessons, Mrs. Stevenson encouraged me to audition for music school at her alma mater, the University of Cincinnati College Conservatory of Music.

Always willing to please, I said yes.

I was often a graceless child. By that I mean not so much a tripping over one's feet, which I certainly did, but a kind of inward awkwardness, a soul hunger that is naïve, subtle, and sometimes crippling. Part of that, of course, is the nature of childhood: the lurch of hormones and questions, the blossom of breasts and habits, the swirl of nagging and tender needs for acceptance and love.

But I mean more than that. Through hard work, charm, and a likable personality, I had an uncommon ability to make a rock smell like a rose, to make excellent grades from what I feared was average intelligence, to cause flagging spirits to rally. I worked hard at achieving a state of grace, honed the craft of transformation with a steely knife that cut both ways—into a warmed heart and a cool void. I pleased until the hunger returned, demanding more.

I was too naïve to know it then. I thought Oreo was a cookie, prejudice only a state of mind. I was sappy and genuine in belief. I thought hard work and love would conquer anything, even the kind of still-distant evil that soaked the headlines and, without my knowing it, every heart.

I did not know then the mechanics of grace. I thought the way any child would think: everything depends on me. I even thought that grace was the product of my own effort. But grace surprised me. It found me, not so much as a warm feeling, but by way of a wound, a pure and razor-like fire. It cut me deeply in ways and places that I least expected.

Once the grace came by music, in the deep movement of pathos. I was a high school junior, saturated in vocal technique and scheduled to sing at a vocal music contest, one of those Saturday affairs held in school basements, where judges hand out I (excellent), II (good), and III (average). On the way over to my music teacher's house, in a huge, two-toned green Oldsmobile, my father and I argued. He accused me of doing something that I didn't do. I tried to explain, to prove my innocence. He cut me off; he wouldn't even listen. The hurt spawned in my silence.

Even as I felt the tears coming, I tried to fight them off. But one or two trickled down my cheek, forcing me to turn my head away from my father and pretend to look out the window so that he could not see me crying. When we got to my teacher's house, I was double-churning over the aria that I was to sing and the pain that I felt. I got out of the car, turned back toward my father, and said chokingly, "I love you, Daddy." I slammed the door on any possible reply that he might have made. I wanted him to know that he had hurt me, and I wanted him to hurt too. I loved him so much, but I hated the walls that he often erected. On the way to the contest with my teacher, I cried and blew my sorrow into a dozen tissues.

When we arrived at the high school where the contest was to be held, I walked to the back of the room and waited. When it was my turn, I walked up, feeling a gray rain inside. I sang, perfect in technique, caught in pathos, unaware of myself. "O Del Mio Dolce Ardor. . . ." Oh, my beloved sweetheart. As I sang, I felt the betrayal the song described, tasted it like grapefruit, and now I heard it captured in a voice that I recognized as my own, bittersweet. Singer and song, love and pain, melded together. A transcendent grace had found my pain and transformed it into beauty. The judges, mesmerized, gave me a I+, the first ever for my high school.

But who can judge such things? Grace always comes from God. In my sophomore year in high school, at Camp Minnewanka, God's penetrating grace found me again. I considered myself a Christian. I had accepted Jesus Christ as my Savior at the age of ten, said the words, believed in my heart, worked for the sun-gold halo stickers, and memorized my Scripture verses. I sang in the choir, seldom missed a Sunday school class, and was deeply impressed with a handful of God's people: their spiritual backbones, the way they stood, leaning slightly, defiantly pure, into the world. But I lived my Christianity the way I lived the rest of my life: needing approval, giving with a full heart, feeling mysteriously half-drained.

But it wasn't until Camp Minnewanka that the reality of God and the weight of his undeserved grace fully hit me. The emphasis of the two-week camp was on fourfold living: mental, emotional, physical, and spiritual. I didn't care too much for the outdoors, with its bugs, heat, and humdrum cabins, but I felt honored to be there, one of three or four picked from the entire school district. I liked to be chosen.

During the first few days, we exercised, explored feelings, competed in games. Somewhere in the middle of the week several hundred girls gathered in a three-sided shelter to hear one of the many speakers. He got up and talked about God, about his voice, about how he comes still, in silence. The speaker talked about how we all talked too much, moved too much, wasted too much even to listen. He challenged us to be still and listen, really listen, after we prayed: "Prayer is a dialogue," I remember him saying, "a *two-way* conversation."

That night I walked out to the beach, stretched out my body on the shore, and put a rock under my head to keep the sand out of my hair. Feeling like Jacob at Bethel, I prayed long and hard, the fire of the stars dancing in a blue-black sky. I felt God's presence. *Lord, I want to be what you want me to be. I don't know what that is or even where I am going, but let me be still enough to listen for your voice.* That was the gist of it. I drained myself,

46

became empty enough to feel weightless, untouched by my own gravity. And I listened. Really listened.

The words came from somewhere—outside of sight, inside my head—but they were as clear as the sky: *You must give yourself to God.* That was it, nothing more. I waited, and in the continuing silence I prayed another prayer, this one prying for a few specifics, a hint of what he wanted me to do.

But that was it. And that was enough. Grace, unexpected and uncoaxed, marked me, set me apart. I felt special, new.

Chosen.

47

*T*yrone was a man of jazz: black, dark, withered like an autumn flower, wasted by a riot of living and cancer. When I first met him, he was uncommunicative and wrapped in pain. His body and spirit spoke of waste: the ruin of alcohol, drugs, and barroom women; the rupture of a family that had disowned him in his negligence. Although he looked to be nearly seventy years old, he was probably closer to fifty.

When I told him I was a music therapist, I saw light in his yellowed eyes. He made an effort to speak through his pain, "I used to be with Miles Davis. Played keyboards for him." I mentioned something about wanting to spend time with such a jazz legend. He sat up in his hospital bed, adjusted the covers, and seemed to grow two inches in stature. As he launched into stories about his time with "his man, Miles," I cupped my hands around my chin and hung on every word. This man, stripped of life and respect, stirred something in me: maybe compassion, maybe pity, maybe the idea of the dignity of human life, no matter how self-embalmed.

Later that week, I pushed a piano over to Tyrone's room. When I asked him if he would show me some of his moves, he balked at first but then gave in. It was hard for him to get out of bed and walk toward the piano; it hurt to watch him struggle. He sat down slowly and took several long breaths. When he lifted his gnarled hands to the keys, a transformation seemed to come over him. It was as dramatic as inflating a flat tire; new life seemed to flow into his body.

He hit the ivory running; his fingers seemed to have a will of their own. From his heart came the jazz forgotten; he was in another world, one that was once filled with pleasure and respect. As he played, I began to sing. One by one the nurses began to gather round this withered man, some swaying, some shouting encouragement, one even climbing on top of the piano. Soon there was a crowd: patients, visitors, janitors, even a few doctors.

Tyrone played for twenty minutes, and then he tired. As the applause rang through the hall, he folded his hands on his lap and his body folded and sank. He drooped into a deflated posture. I could see in those shrinking moments that he longed for the way things used to be.

Chapter Three

The College Years: The Discipline of Dreaming

***Sforzando** (forcibly with sudden emphasis)*

Chosen. I think of Israel, wrestled-over Jacob, under the damning mercy of the law, the poorest of all nations. Yet God chose him. I think of myself, believing that I can be good enough, pure enough, and obedient enough. Yet God chose me, me with my puny IQ of 106.

Chosen. Among hundreds of applications, following a nerve-splitting audition, I was selected to be a voice major by the University of Cincinnati College Conservatory of Music in the summer of 1966. It was an honor, one that I felt called to prove. For the next four years, I worked to merit the grandiosity of the gesture, to keep the illusion of self-worth alive.

I feared the secret that I privately held: I was unworthy and incapable. I worked myself into a frenzy, and by the third quarter of my first year I found myself exhausted, anemic, and mainlining vitamin B by doctor's order. I wrestled with choosing a major. My voice teacher, Lucille Evans, held up to me her standard: music-performance students are artist and elite, the chosen of the chosen. My parents, on the other hand, wanted me to graduate with a degree that would have some pragmatic value, like music education, which was more given to daily bread than transcendent flash. Yet my parents never dictated to me what I should do; rather they allowed me to make my own choice and assured me of their support. Even in their pragmatism, they knew the value of dreaming and the incalculable cost of a broken dream. Above all, they did not want me to look back on my life and have regrets.

I decided to take both majors, music performance and music education: one for her, one for them, and, in my need to please, nothing for me.

In order to be able to graduate in four years with a double major, I took eighteen to twenty-two extra credit hours per quarter, worked a part-time job, and burned out. In my creeping fatigue even I knew that I could not maintain my pace and my sanity. I could handle only one major. At the start of my sophomore year, I chose music performance. The decision was the result of much prayer, a battery of career and personality tests, and the memory of the I+ from my high school solo-and-ensemble contest, when God filled me with a pure and flawless flow of music. I wanted more of those mesmerizing moments. By choosing music performance, I was hoping to calculate the formula that would make such grace last.

Not everyone weathered the demands of college. The conservatory, if nothing else, taught me that music took not only heart and the whim of feeling but also discipline. Technique—the breathing, the diaphragm, the throat, the stance—was calculated to pull the string of voice through the body until I could sing out the top of my head, effortlessly. Art was the chemistry of interpretation and technique, and when those two were balanced, they could transport a song and the singer into another realm, another perspective. Art, in a sense, was the discipline of emotion.

The endless discipline demanded that I live for art, the obsession of perfection. Those who would settle for less would quit, flunk, transfer, or consider a biology major. The pressure—a swirl of endless practice and intense competition—threatened to eat me alive, cut me in half at the spleen. The external pressure was internalized at the level of marrow, ligament, and soul.

I didn't know if I could manage the pressure. My scholarship demanded that I maintain at least a 3.0 grade-point average. I was competing for grades and recognition with many students who were better prepared, who had studied music theory, who had been schooled overseas, prepped by masters, preened from birth for a career in music. I, on the other hand, had wanted to be a nurse until my high school voice teacher suggested that I give music a try. In contrast to other students, I entered the conservatory with a this-is-going-to-be-great attitude.

I don't think I would have made it without my roommate and best friend for four years. We shared a great deal. She also began at the conservatory in the fall of 1966, the only other black female student in our dorm. In addition, we were both from lower-middle-income families, riding scholarships, connected to values, family, and pragmatism. We were roomed together, I suspect, because we were both black. In 1966, I don't suppose it was a coincidence.

What we didn't share, we sharpened in one another. In as many ways that we found comfort in common ground, we also were different. She was the confident one, majoring in music education, which in the conservatory pecking order was perceived to be of secondary importance; I, the insecure one, majored in music performance, considered to be reserved for the crème de la crème. She taught me about self-confidence, and she learned from me discipline.

Her singing voice was intense, high, pretty, and precise. I wasn't overwhelmed as much by her talent as her stamina; she had a voice that never seemed to tire. She could sing for three hours or more and sound as if she had just begun. I was not so fortunate. Although she once told me that my singing voice was the most beautiful voice she had heard, I lacked endurance; my voice would falter within an hour. She was powerful in technique; I was not.

From our strengths and weaknesses, we learned how to compensate. What my friend lacked in raw ability, she made up for in presence of command and popularity. Unlike me, she was secure in herself, firm in saying no, not captive to grades and titles. Voted the Alpha Sweetheart, she was unwilling to be driven by the needs and whims of others. What I lacked in technique, I sought to overcome with discipline, art, interpretation, and drive.

She and I were, in many ways, a reflection of my sister and me, the two unique halves that made a whole. We shared family. One Christmas, my parents had sacrificed and bought me an expensive pair of butter-soft, over-the-calf, brown leather boots. They were sharp! When I returned to school with my parents, my roommate and her parents were in our room. The first thing I wanted to do was to show off my new boots. "You're not going to believe it, girl. Get ready for this. Take a look at what my mom and dad got me." The language was ambiguous and could have been taken for good or bad.

When I pulled out the boots, her father said sympathetically, "It's all right, honey, you just wear those boots anyway. You don't have to be ashamed." My friend and I looked at each other, stunned for a second, inwardly giggling.

"Well, thank you, sir," I said politely.

We had our private jokes because we needed our sense of humor to outdistance the pace of our lives. *You just wear them anyway.* We would say it to each other often, in encouragement or warning, in the blast of pressure.

The conservatory drained me. I felt I had to practice longer and study harder than most of the other students, many of whom were formally trained. The same external needs for achievement and approval drove me to succeed. I wasn't satisfied unless I had As. I was determined to please my parents. But beyond that I was driven by an internal need: I wanted excellence for the sake of excellence and demanded the best of myself. Flaws were not to be despised but studied and corrected, yielding another direction to perfection. When I saw others do better, I worked that much harder; not necessarily to be better than they were, but to acknowledge that there was still room for improvement and more hard work.

The conservatory's curriculum was stacked to move from theory to application. In other words, the classes that provided a foundation of thought, philosophy, and context—like theory analysis, Western civilization, music history—generally came during the first two years; the classes that dealt more directly with performance—composition, conducting, harmony, pedagogy—were taken during the final two years. The curriculum increased in difficulty over time.

I struggled from the beginning. During the spring quarter of my sophomore year, I took my first music-theory class, which involved the precise, mathematical study of music. I was rattled. How could such beauty, such purity in space and time, be analyzed? Broken down like a high school biology frog, music was dissected into chords and melody, lines and climaxes, the inner guts and workings of what often defies description. Its pragmatism bordered on sacrilege for me, a tinkering with the atoms of an invisible force. Diminution, augmentation, chromatic modulations, hypomixolydian retrograde melodies, scales, half notes, quarter notes, eighth notes, the movement of the big picture into stringy ligaments of understanding.

The constant fragmentation of music into its lowest common terms, the analysis of the thoughts of a composer, the intellectual speculation of great art often undermined the very beauty that was supposed to be merely experienced. At the same time the broken-down elements of music taught me of its complexity and produced within me a fresh awe of its dimension and power.

I might have had an easier time with this kind of science if I would not have had a crazy man for my first music-theory class. By himself, he made my sophomore year a nightmare. As a portion of one final exam, for example, he would have four singers sing a cappella in four-part harmony and ask the students to transcribe their singing, note for note. What made the task even more difficult was that the singers were not accurate in pitch. We would sit there, in red-eyed disbelief, and wonder if this man might have been skipping his medication. He seemed heartless, out of touch, almost cruel. He was gone in a couple of years, sometime after the students took a ten-foot marble bust of Mozart, risking hernias and expulsion, and lodged Wolfgang next to this man's front door. Transcribe *that*. Before he departed, however, he left me, along with more than half the class, with my first D ever, a permanent smudge on my academic record and pride.

Although the classes moved in a progression, the practice, voice lessons, and performing were never-ending. From the time students enrolled as first-year students until they graduated (or dropped out or failed), they were locked into a three- or four-hour-a-day regimen: the training of the vocal cords, lungs, and mind. I practiced vocaleze—the running up and down of scales—to increase my range, endurance, and flexibility. I practiced songs, mostly in foreign languages, looking up each word in the appropriate dictionary, which sometimes yielded insight, sometimes gibberish. Interpretation demanded understanding. If I was singing an aria from an opera, I needed to know the whole story, the depth of my character.

In the movement, the pace, the blinding need to prove and improve myself, I could not see where I was headed. But still I pressed on, crying when I needed to or phoning my parents to connect with the love and acceptance that I understood best. I was determined to succeed, to make people proud of me, to slip beyond my limits, both real and imagined.

My passion and drive often turned humorous. In college I learned early of God's sense of humor, the beauty of a laugh. During our first quarter, I was taking violin lessons to fulfill our instrumental-methods requirement. My violin methods course met at eight o'clock each Saturday morning; I often practiced on Friday night. I dressed very informally at night: long johns, flannels, pink socks, that type of thing—not exactly dressed for the four-color spreads of *Vogue*. When I practiced violin, I would slip down to the basement level of the dorm, where I could play without disturbing other students.

On one particular night, I headed off to the basement, looking especially disheveled, almost clownish: pajamas, housecoat, socks, flip-flop slippers, rolled hair, and to keep the curlers in place, a pair of panties on my head. Do you get the picture? I practiced Bach or one of the other masters, hair curlers punching through the leg holes of my panties, for a couple of hours, until about one o'clock in the morning. When I returned to the elevator and pressed the button, my stomach sank. The elevator, I recalled, did not go down to the basement. The only way back to my twelfth-floor room was to go outside and enter through the front door of the dorm. Twelve inches of snow covered the ground, and on the long steps to the door, couples were kissing good-bye, somewhat oblivious to my Bozo-the-Clown number.

I took a deep breath and marched through the snow, my flip-flops like pink little shovels, *crip, crip, crip,* and headed for the door in hurried steps. Since it was after midnight, I had to stand and knock, waiting for a security guard to open the door. I could hear the snickers all around me, but I tried to be cool, as if it were autumn, as if I were walking casually in the woods and didn't really have panties on my head.

The guard in his official blue-creased uniform opened the door and stepped back when I entered. This was, judging by the look on his face and his stunned silence, an apparition that would come back to visit him in the future, after pizza at night or after too much caffeine. I walked past this man, not the least bit sympathetic to his future hauntings, and making eye contact with no one, I rushed to the elevator and up to my room. My roommate had just returned from a date, and when she saw me, she burst into uncontrollable, howling laughter. I finally stepped back from my bruised pride and caught a glimpse of myself in the mirror. I joined her in her temporary insanity.

That was just like us. We often laughed until we cried. Like the time we sang together in this hotsy-totsy, we-have-money wedding. Feeling quite out of place at the reception, we amused ourselves by imitating inebriated gentlemen, properly drunk, full of themselves. We were in our element, and private laughter surrounded us. We cackled like two hens.

Or I remember the time we were in a building together when I had to make an emergency trip to the rest room. The building looked vacant, so I decided to go into the men's rest room, which was close at hand. As I was finishing my business, I heard the outside door open. I quickly put my feet up on the toilet, hoping, praying, that he wouldn't open my stall. Whoever it was—I'm assuming it was a "he" and not another misplaced female—chose the stall next to me. My legs began to cramp as I sat there still as a mouse, waiting until he left the stall, washed his hands, and combed his hair. Finally I heard the outside door close. As I came out of the men's room, we both exploded in laughter.

She had a knack for bringing me back to reality. In many ways I must have appeared as contradictory. Even while I constantly analyzed and hammered at perfection, I stumbled when I danced, and felt, in a sense, that the panties were always on top of my head. Like any good friend, she had a gift of pulling me out of myself and showed me with a laugh not to take myself so seriously.

It was at the conservatory, in the music, that I discovered that I could turn it on. During my final two years of college, I learned that I had a knack for performance. At the drop of a hat or with the correct break of a smile, I could assume a persona. Even through my limitations, I performed well.

During my junior year, I landed a small part in the comic opera *Gianni Schicchi*. My character was trying to impress a wealthy man, who was about to leave a large fortune to some fortunate person. My character had to attempt to compensate for a screwy little husband, who confused up with down, who most certainly harbored a low IQ. About two weeks before the opera debuted, I started thinking about my character: who she was, how to play her, how to *be* her. With study, concentration, and a bit of daring, I charmed and pulled that character out of my heart.

Our coach for the opera was Italo Tajo, an internationally famous Metropolitan Opera star, who always had about him a hint of fresh garlic. I wanted to impress him, a man rich in talent and discernment. When I started acting, becoming the character, he was astounded. Once he stopped rehearsal and exclaimed, "Look at zis! Look at vat Deforia is doing!" He stopped, working up another rave, and came over and pinched my cheeks, "Vat you ahr doing, vat you ahr doing. Zo good."

I didn't know what I was doing; it happened through daring, discipline, and instinct, the birthing of art, approval. It was then I realized that I had been right in choosing music performance as my major. In a loose sort of oxymoron, I could feel the tension of the truth: turning it on, inspired. That's the way music, good music, usually is: studied, ordered, performed.

Great music, the kind that soars, is much rarer. Through me, it happens so seldom: in a high school basement and once or twice at the conservatory. In my junior year, I landed the lead in the Puccini opera *Suor Angelica*. My character was a girl who gave birth to an illegitimate child and was sent off during her pregnancy to a convent. I felt for her, deeply, almost as if she were a part of me: a probing or prophetic voice. I always had a connection for the neglected, the souls that seemed to be disconnected, feeling outside of grace. Here was the ultimate hurt and hope: a woman of God, good as a nun, marked with a scarlet letter of sin. Will she ever be clean, graceful, and grace-filled? Or will she stumble, a two-left-footed soul, into the churning of doubt and rejection?

This part was the high note, the high note of high notes, the glorious climax. It was the fulfillment of every soprano's dreams: the spotlight in a magnificent aria that captures victory and voice. My chance came one night near the end of the opera when the young woman expresses how sorry she is to her illegitimate baby, whom she has never seen, and to God. She is on bended knee, arms outstretched, looking heavenward, invoking forgiveness. At the end of the aria the high A note comes and is allowed to linger on the breath, in the air, charged and subtle.

I usually choke on high notes, try too hard, crack the words in my pinched throat. Not on this night. The note soared, walked through the air on its own, like the winged prayer of a child. Without exaggeration, in a real magic, we were all caught up in that note: singer, audience, instrumentalists, musicians, all of us. When it was over, a time suspended and faded, there was no applause, only silence.

It wasn't a performance. Not really. There was in that note the learning of technique all right—my exercised vocal cords, my endless vocaleze, my proper stance, even my D grade in music theory. But it was more than that. There was in that note the study of character: the swim of emotion, the pumping of blood. But it was more than that. There was in that note, me, a precious part of me, up from down deep, a pearl in the bottomless sea. But it was more than that. I was, in the best sense of the word, used. Used like the banks of a river are used by water. By an arrangement of grace.

They never seemed to last, these transcendent moments, and I was left to calculate why. Was I restricted by my talent, by my musical limitations, which I knew even then were real, few, and toxic to my chosen career? And could I overcome, learn to plumb the depths of approval, ride the peak notes more often?

I was hooked on the idea of transformation. It is why, as a child, I dreamed of being a healer. At the conservatory, I began to see in music the power to transform at deeper levels, to touch hearts and souls. I had tasted of the power of music to captivate, mesmerize, and change. I was hooked on the pure grace of it.

But so were most of the other students. Competition became the name of the game. In order to rise to such heights, others had to descend into obscurity or failure. All of us at the conservatory knew the pecking order. At the bottom rung were the music education students, who, like my roommate, were viewed as safe, unwilling to risk their futures to the art of music. They were craftspeople and teachers, not artists. They were pragmatists, not dreamers. They wanted, first and foremost, to have a job to do.

Music performance, while above music education, was not without its own social order. Students in theater performance, while artists, were viewed (wrongly) as somewhat unrefined, wild, guttural, the musical equivalent of velvet Elvises. They were laid back and natural, more appealing than those training in the classics, and determined to dance their voices into ear candy and probably, what with the rush of it all, into oblivion.

Those who studied classical music were the crème de la crème, the way they milked the masters, smiled high-white smiles. They were cultured, paced, and controlled. They were quintessential artists.

If I ever believed in this scale of worth, which I did not, my roommate balanced me. She was a music education major, committed to what was important, anchored in the reality of who she was and where she came from. Neither one of us had much money. In order to audition successfully, properly, we needed the appropriate dress. I remember she and I were allowed to go and pick out dresses that rich women had donated to the conservatory. We were like two little girls in a basement kingdom, trying on our mother's clothes. The sheer grandiosity of it left us giggling.

But I knew it never fit, this brilliant disguise. I was a misfit of sorts, black for one thing, not particularly fond of white gloves, wanting even less to sing to a theater full of them. I was uncomfortable with those who in their pride mistook weightlessness as having risen to the top. At the same time I was not exactly anchored in selflessness. My insecurity needed constant feeding, a steady diet of approval, applause, success in its most limited terms.

The simple fact was: I had to survive. There were only so many chances, so many parts, so many dreams to be realized. Every year, we had to sing before a jury made up of voice faculty, who would evaluate our individual progress. That performance, combined with grades, determined whether we would continue at the conservatory. A half-hour could ruin a life.

I remember specifically the jury between my sophomore and junior years. For weeks, I practiced and practiced, prepar-

59

ing for the three of four songs that I might be asked to sing. The night before this particular jury I remember singing outside, in the pitch black, feeling my voice give out on me. I always had a difficult time discerning between the need to prepare fully and the need to push myself beyond my limits. At the audition, the jury members sat scattered throughout the stage, holding clipboards, ranking, scoring, and evaluating each student's musicianship, technique, interpretation, and stage appearance. They sat for hours and hours.

I remember standing in the hall outside the auditorium, my throat dry, and wondering why it was taking each student so long. As each student came through the door, I intently examined his or her face for some kind of sign as to the judges' states of mind. Finally I went on stage, performed my songs and left. I had to wait a week for the results, at my next voice lesson. I passed the test, and though their scores indicated specific areas that needed improvement, the judges' comments reflected that they clearly saw me and my voice as promising.

Even then the audition and the grades were not enough. Progressing in the world of the conservatory was also based on intangibles: the person with whom you studied, the difficulty of the pieces, who recommended whom, who auditioned where, the length of a future resume. These were often the stepping stones to someone else's dream. We measured each other by the marks we made. At the same time we found a sense of community in the intensity of the competition: a shared sense of music, beauty, and spiritual hunger.

With me, it wasn't so much a desire to rise above everyone else but to keep from sinking down into myself. I was afraid that if I let up, even for a second, I would drown in a blue fear, my secret pool of insufficiency. I was afraid of myself, of stopping to be who I was, and of scarring the pretty picture that others would often paint of me.

So I busied myself in success. I won awards, scholarships, and parts. During the summers of my junior and senior years, I performed with the Cincinnati Opera Company, singing in the choir of such operas as *Mefistofele*, *Carmen*, and *Rigoletto*. I was called back for second auditions with the Santa Fe and Metropolitan Opera companies. I sometimes gave my teachers goose bumps. I did summer stock in Kentucky, even a theater production, and I found in acting that same stop-time connection with something beyond myself. Between my junior and senior years, my coach, Sylvia Olden Lee, suggested that I was good enough to try out for the traveling company performing *Porgy and Bess*. But partly because of a fear of failure and partly because I did not want to take a year away from school, I decided not to audition.

Even in the middle of the awards and accolades hovered the doubt, a haunting spirit of discernment. At times I felt as if I were faking it.

I remember vividly one particular competition, an annual scholarship contest, for which about twenty students competed. I decided to sing a Puccini aria, comparatively lightweight, romantic, schmaltzy. If nothing else, I knew how to play to my strengths, to maximize the sweet. I won the scholarship. After the contest a black student, whom I had known to be pleasant enough, came up to me and said, "I should have won that contest. They gave it to you because they didn't want to give it to me." He had performed a technically more difficult number and genuinely felt he should have won. I was perpetually fragile, and with this brother in my face, I felt despondent, defensive, shattered. I crumbled underfoot. I knew he may have been right.

In the long run, I didn't think I would make it. Underneath the God-given beauty of natural talent, a flair for interpretation, and an ongoing performance, I knew that I was limited in technique. My voice may have been gifted, but I didn't know what to do with it. I would often be confused by the mechanics, by the making of the sound. I couldn't consistently get the sound to that certain end-place in my head. Sometimes I had to fake it.

On another level, I simply lacked the vocal ammunition. I often choked on high notes, especially under pressure, and lacked stamina and mobility. After an hour or two, I would run out of gas and my voice would weary; I could not run arpeggios with speed *and* grace. No matter how great my interpretation, I sensed that I could not redefine the eventuality of my fate. I feared that my career in music, at least in this chosen form, was headed down a dead-end road.

Even early on in my schooling I intuitively sensed my limitations. I wondered where all of this was going to lead. The fear drove me to take a psychological test designed to determine what career a person was best qualified to do. The test revealed that I was equally proficient to be a performer, a teacher, or a nun. I have never been good at multiple choice, and certainly not when it was my heart that was spread into so many: (a) corners, (b) uncertainties, (c) fears. Probably all of the above. But that was not allowed.

I knew that whatever I did, I would do in service to God. Ever since that day at Camp Minnewanka, lying Jacob-like on the stone pillow on a night beach, I was convinced that my life would be marked for God. His voice had been so clear, so audible. I longed now for such concrete direction, such a holy path to follow.

The voice that I heard was less divine, not my own. My last vocal coach at the conservatory, Sylvia Olden Lee, had encouraged me to audition for acceptance at the Curtis Institute of Music, an institution rivaled only by the Julliard School of Music. As I had done four years earlier, I acquiesced. I had no other plans; I agreed to try out.

The next voice was closer to divine, at least in the eyes of the music world. It belonged to Max Rudolph, the conductor for the Cincinnati Symphony Orchestra and previous conductor of the Prague Orchestra and the Metropolitan Opera Company. Maestro Rudolph, prompted by my coach, asked me to his house to help prepare the three or four arias that I might be asked to sing at my audition for the Curtis Institute. This was a privilege beyond my wildest dreams, and for a while it tamed my fears; it felt like the gravity of direction.

During the final quarter of my senior year at the Cincinnati Conservatory, I auditioned for acceptance at the Curtis Institute of Music. The pressure was immense:

Rittenhouse Square, the plush blue auditorium seats, high ceilings, mahogany woodwork, the grand chandeliers, the five precise judges sitting beyond the lights in judgment, measuring my worth in twenty minutes. They asked me to sing arias. "Senza Mama," from the opera *Suor Angelica;* I failed to soar to transcendent heights, as I had before, but I was certainly credible. Then they gave me a Bach aria, whose title I can't remember, and I clutched, finally froze. I hadn't practiced it since my senior recital, didn't believe they would ask me to sing it. I started once, then twice, drawing a blank at the same spot, feeling I had been wounded in my psyche, bleeding red embarrassment until it pooled and stained the precious dignity of their time, their starched white presence.

From the distance, like carefully measured thunder, came a judge's voice: "Young lady," he said, "if you really want to do this, come back tomorrow, knowing the music." I turned and walked off the stage, humiliated. I remember going somewhere on a subway, sunk in rage, devastated not so much by embarrassment or rejection but by the tone in the voice of one of the other judges. My anger, not often kindled, lingered in his nasal bleating, the eloquence and ease at which he sacrificed my feelings. *I'm going home to my momma and daddy,* I remember thinking. *I don't have to let these people bother me.*

The next day I returned to the stage, not caring how I did. I was poised, not looking any of the judges in the eye, singing past them, in myself. Released from my fear, I sang with dignity, purpose, beauty. My judges were impressed. I again walked off the stage, this time having remembered every word. Not caring about their approval, I was accepted into the esteemed Curtis Institute of Music. I could begin in the fall of 1970, with full tuition paid. It cost me only a willingness to fail.

My roommate and I graduated in 1970 from the conservatory. Dressed in our red robes, hats and tassels, we marched down the aisle, but again, we headed in different directions. Always secure in the movement of her life, she had already decided to go on to graduate school; I was undecided.

That graduation day was filled with extremes of joy and uncertainty. Even among the hundreds of faces, I found my parents in the crowd and waved. I saw in their faces the look of pride (their first daughter graduating from college) and secret concern (What would Deforia do now?). Even with the diploma in my hand, I also felt, in between the hugs of congratulations and shouts of joy, a piercing silence.

Months later as I packed to move to the Curtis Institute, sanctioned in approval, soon to be rubbing shoulders with important musicians, the pragmatist in me wondered what I was doing and where it was leading. What good would come of it? The dreamer in me would answer, *Was not this God's open door, this perfect chasm?*

The Curtis Institute swallowed me. It was not so much the poor grades in counterpoint, the ear training, the inability to hear something and sing it back or write it down. It was not so much the sight singing, the transposing, the cognitive havoc of a short circuit between my brain, heart, and fingers. It wasn't even so much that we, my vocal coach and I, were trying to fix what could not be fixed. It was more the swallowing itself. Those who *had it*, sometimes consciously but mostly naturally, swallowed those who *didn't have it*. That's about as simple as I can say it.

It, I believe, is a condition of the mind or spirit, in any case something that rides below the surface, fueling on vast quantities of energy, focus, God only knows what. *Intensity* might be the word that comes closest. Those who taught, as well as those who absorbed, all had *it*. You could see it in their eyes—a mind racing too fast for all the possibilities; a devouring spirit of perfectionism; the magnetic repelling of those who could not break into that certain space.

I would try, really try, to follow along. More often than not, my most demanding teachers were those who taught in arenas in which I was least competent. But even then I felt some hope. After an entire year of fixing, I was finally getting somewhere.

I was grasping, in a stiff sort of way, proper technique. My teacher, Ellen Rulau, who heard right away what I was missing, sought to make up for four years of compensating by breaking down all that I had learned earlier. She worked to give me new images so that I could get the proper mental picture of what was really going on. That picture, she said, had to come before the sensation. Otherwise, I would always have to wait on just the right moment.

I labored feverishly, but for the first time in my life, the work ethic failed me. The end came quickly, within ten minutes maybe, before a mandatory end-of-year jury. I walked on stage, nodded to a pianist whom I had never seen before, started singing, and watched the judges look around, chew pencils, break my heart. Within a short time, I received a letter: I would not be coming back to the Curtis Institute of Music.

The first thing I did was talk to my teacher. "I thought we were finally getting somewhere," I said to her. "We were finally moving forward."

In a gentle way, she said as she read the letter, "Honey, I'm sorry. But there comes a time when you have to move on to something else." She was trying to tell me, *Deforia, cut it loose.*

After I left her office, I went to a rest room, sat in a stall, and cried. Five years of work, of pouring myself out, for what? After about thirty minutes, I finally settled. As I stood up to leave the stall, I realized that the back of my skirt had fallen in the toilet. I walked out of the rest room, bearing the unmistakable mark of a person who was no longer in control of herself. How could a twenty-three-year-old woman, looking to all the world as if she had just wet herself, ever be mistaken for a picture of God's grace?

I was confused and embarrassed.

Rejected.

That same evening, a Friday in May of 1971, I talked to my parents. They had sacrificed so much, for what? We chatted first of superficial things—the weather, the blossom of a garden. Then I told them the results of my audition. I wouldn't be coming back for a second year. More than anything else, I hated disappointing my parents. They didn't say much, except that they loved me no matter what. They told me to pack my bags and come home. And that was enough. I remember it was rainy and gray, inside and out, and in the chill of failure, I felt like anything but spring.

A day later I had an appointment with Rudolf Serkin, the director of the Curtis Institute. For once in my life I decided against quiet complacency and wanted to be assertive. The building that housed the director's office was reminiscent of an old, proud mansion: gleaming cherry and mahogany wood, brass trim, historic paintings, tapestry on the walls. Up a long, winding staircase to Serkin's office, I practiced my lines. *I was trying. Things were just starting to click. I knew that if I were given another chance and another year, I could do it, even if it required every ounce of my energy.* My words were simple, passionate, and urgent.

Serkin was gentle and smiled. "Deforia," he said, "don't measure your worth on whether you can return to the Curtis Institute. You are more than this." I remember a warm, gentle hand on my shoulder and the feeling that I was talking to a man with extraordinary vision. He knew, it seemed, something about which I could only guess.

A year or so later, after losing track of her, I got a call from my roommate. She told me that she had been taken under the wing of Thomas Shippers, a famous conductor, and was scheduled in a series of performances across the country. The one who had preferred pragmatism to performance had been chosen. She would soon sing for presidents and popes—possessing the half that I lacked, she was about to become a superstar.

And what was to become of me? How could I predict my future when I knew so little about myself in the present?

For years, Elonna had waited. Finally, God answered her prayer. She gave birth—to five children, all at the same time.

It soon seemed a flawed miracle, however. One of the babies died, and while Elonna was in the hospital, she was diagnosed with an inoperable, terminal cancer.

I remember meeting Elonna for the first time. Elonna was a Christian. She told me how she had endured years of infertility and, after taking a fertility drug, finally became pregnant. She and her husband had rejoiced at the news. And now this. Within five minutes, unlike my usual professional self, I was crying. We sang hymns together and talked of God's will. I was able to calm her.

I was much less effective with her newborns. When I sang and played for them, one passed gas, another spit up, another fell asleep, and only one followed my voice with eye contact. Day after day, I would get the same reactions.

I would go home, sometimes, and cry. "How could God do this?" I asked my husband. Give life, at long last, and take life so quickly. They gave Elonna six months to live. But Elonna defied the odds: she was discharged from the hospital, chose to take alternative treatments, and is alive today with her family.

Quackery, some would say, and mystery. Elonna, though, attributes her healing to an unproved drug and to the unseen hand of God—who can, through faith, make the impossible possible.

Chapter Four

The Early Adult Years: Dying to Live

Staccato (detached)

*M*en. They were people I knew, talked to, shook hands with, but no one, especially at a dance, to step out with. If grace were a woman at a dance, she would not wear size eleven shoes. Like me. I spent most of my early adult years resigned to my role as the wallflower, hidden in the corner, my large feet tucked under the chair.

Occasionally a male came by to pick the wallflower. Like Rick Roberson, the University of Cincinnati Bearcats' basketball star. When he asked me to dance, I blushed red, felt the color move through my veins. I could only look up, feel my neck crick like the crack of knuckles: six-foot-eight-inches tall, dimples, and a Pillsbury-Doughboy kind of cool. It was a slow dance, of all things. So there I was, moving my feet as if they were untripped mines, bruising his feet and my pride. He was slick as ice and tried to reassure me with his slow words: "It's okay, baby. Now where have you been, girl?" He set me down after the dance, said a few smooth words, and glided across the floor, forever out of sight, and me, alone, the wallflower wilting in low light.

I remember another dance, when from my wallflower

corner I saw another man, as big as the bass in a drum, heading in my direction. I had noticed him from across the room, putting on glasses to scan the room, finding someone, taking his glasses off, and making a beeline in my direction. I felt my heart miss a beat, then pound in rhythm. There he was, a man in command, asking for a dance—asking the girl next to me, that is. I stood there while they danced, he and she, wanting it to be us, him and me, and all the while a fever danced in my head. After the dance was over, he walked her back and started talking to me, even put his glasses back on, as if he was afraid he would lose sight of a word. And that was it; no invitation to dance, no hint of a smile, not even a funny slip of the tongue, just casual language, the kind you might use on an airplane 40,000 feet over the Rockies. *High and mighty*, I thought. *The nerve*.

This was the man, the man who did not ask me to dance, who would become my husband. I would have never guessed it then, hot in anger and cool in grace, that a man named Ernest, with a temperament to match, would sweep me off my feet and later deny it was he who had asked the girl standing next to me for a dance.

A few months later he was standing next to me in the campus art gallery. I had gone there to escape the pressures of final exams and prerecital jitters. "You're Deforia, aren't you?" he asked. I think, but have no solid proof, that he was more interested in my yellow jumpsuit than in any great work of art. We struck up a conversation. As it turned out, he had visited my home church in Dayton and knew the Bonners, Kilborns, and Wests, friends of my family. He had seen me sing at the church. I knew of him, not with a name to a face, but I had heard of him indirectly.

It was an easy conversation. I learned that he was a student at the University of Cincinnati College of Design, Architecture, and Art (DAA) and wanted to be an architect. He was also enrolled in ROTC (Reserve Officer Training Corps). I noticed a certain chemistry, an almost quantifiable glow between us. And then suddenly he turned and walked away, saying "I'll call you sometime." I was a bit put off, the heat in the head thing again, and wondered why he cut it off so quickly when the conversation was flowing so smoothly.

As I was walking back to my dorm, I saw another student from the DAA, one whom I had had my eye on for quite some time. This was the guy I had secretly named Mr. Dreamboat. He was soft-spoken, good-looking, smart. I had a thing for him from a distance. He stopped me and wanted to talk. What was this—two handsome men talking to me in the same day after a dry spell that would make walking in the Sahara seem like an ocean cruise? The yellow jumpsuit, maybe, the way it was striped at the pockets, the way it colored my confidence, zipped up the front? Mr. Dreamboat and I had a wonderful conversation, but then again I would have interpreted two words from him as a Magna Carta, a promise of things to come. He also said he would call me.

I almost ran back to my dorm room, ready to stake out a place by my phone. A few hours passed and, sure enough, my phone rang. I let it ring a few times, trying not to appear overly anxious, my nerves jangled. We talked for over an hour. It wasn't, "Hey, babe. How you doin'?" And it wasn't overly intellectual, just warm heart-to-heart conversation: current events, music, architecture, food, church, college, the future. He was stimulating, refreshing, challenging, humorous, and not full of himself. We laughed a lot. He was everything I had imagined him to be, and more.

Mr. Dreamboat, I thought. Then suddenly the conversation took an awkward and unexpected turn. "My mother is calling me to dinner. I have to go." I thought it was one of his jokes, but his tone of voice remained serious. I knew that he lived in a dorm and that he must have come from across the world.

"Is your mother visiting you?" I asked, confused.

"No, she lives here. We all do." And then it hit me: this was not Mr. Dreamboat; it was Ernest. Ernest, the man who didn't ask me to dance, the man who cut short our conversation earlier that afternoon. Straight, direct, living-at-home Ernest.

When I thought he was Mr. Dreamboat, he had swept me

off my feet. Charmed, I found him to be charming. Our relationship took off. Ernest and I started dating six weeks before the end of our studies at the University of Cincinnati. During the summer, we corresponded as he left for an ROTC camp in Pennsylvania, and I landed a summer job with the Cincinnati Opera Company. In the fall of 1970, when I was accepted at the Curtis Institute of Music in Pennsylvania, he was stationed at an army base near Fort Belvoir, Virginia. He was only hours away; he drove a couple of hundred miles once a month so that we could see each other.

I fell in love with Ernest. There is no question about that. Yet it was a love continually overwhelmed with infatuation. Our attraction sprung from both what we shared and how we differed. He, like me, was the child of a blue-collar working man, who worked a milling machine. He, like me, was fed oatmeal and black-eyed peas and the work ethic, a solid diet of fiber, value, discipline, and sturdy living. His father, like mine, was precise and easy-going, with folds in his clothes that could have creased the pages of a magazine. His mother, a housewife, was energetic, giving, and creative: she crocheted, painted, worked with ceramics, and sewed. She was vocal and respected, a veritable Dear Abby of her world of church, community, and home. Ernest had a brother, ten years younger, who died at the age of twelve of a heart condition. The Lane family, like mine, was rooted in God and church.

Similar upbringings, like children nursed on the same milk, do not always produce the same results. In many ways Ernest and I couldn't have been more different. Where I was extroverted, insecure, and swayed by others, he was quiet, strong, and opinionated. Where I had no idea what I was going to do with my life, he had his plotted and charted, *i*'s dotted and *t*'s crossed, a detailed draft of the future. Where I was trying to find my identity, he exuded strength of character and purpose. Where my voice clenched under pressure, he spoke with authority. Those things were attractive to me: those things that were everything I wasn't.

It's not that we were complete opposites. Far from it. We

were on the same wavelength, in much the same way that blue and orange are at the same time both antagonistic and complementary: merely on different sides of the same color wheel. We both, at the spot of color or soul, desired a certain definition of grace, a longing for beauty and sturdiness of purpose. We just took different paths, through different temperaments, in different styles.

Perhaps the difference was also reflected in the professions we had chosen: architecture and opera. Both in a sense burn with the same vision: a fluidity of lines and the concrete expression of what is ethereal or transcendent—art, beauty, grace, whatever you want to call it. Yet there is a world of difference between a blueprint and a song. There is a contrast in vision, in what each sees, in how it is seen. Architecture, it seems to me, relies on external focus, a mapping of what is or should be out there; a blueprint is the etching of facts. Internal realities are necessary only to accomplish the job at hand; they are tools, if you will. Opera, on the other side of the color wheel, is focused internally, in what moves in the soul, a rummaging of what might be or what could be, a tour of the heart's scenery. What lies outside is by no means irrelevant, but secondary, at best.

An architect with a plan and a singer without a clue. I can see now that it was a dangerous love, volatile in its possibilities, quiet in its hints of friction. I could find no wrong in Ernest. It wasn't just that I was awed by his focused intensity; I also felt a certain fusion, a touch maybe, that connected us, flesh and bone and heart. He could access in me places where no one had ever been before—with a raise of an eyebrow, a memory of disappointment or hope, the way he held my hand or listened to my laugh. In the control, I sensed a vulnerability, a willingness to be heard and to hear. Although he would seldom bare his soul, he would toss out a bit of himself at a time, pieces to the puzzle.

In the winter of 1970, on one of his visits to see me at the Curtis Institute, we were engaged. "Let's go look for rings," he said. That was it. No proposal. No dropping to one knee. Just the kind of bold words that I loved. It was so casual, so non-descript, in fact, that I can't even remember the date.

We were officially engaged, and I was on the phone to my parents blurting out, "Ernest has something he wants to say to you." We didn't set a date; both of us wanted me to finish school first.

When I was not accepted for a second year at the Curtis Institute in 1971, I decided to return to the University of Cincinnati, work as a dorm counselor, finish a master's degree in a year, and then get married. That was our blueprint. Even Ernest, as calculated as he could be, thought it would work.

It was an old building, a house that had become a clinic. I found it convenient that I should go there; it was on campus. It was close to Christmas break, one quarter into my master's degree, another three remaining. I was businesslike when I asked for the test.

A few minutes later, they sat me in a small room with old magazines to wait for the results. "The Intimacy Factor." "The Sexual Revolution." "Models with Flair Pants." "Richard Nixon." The music may have been John Denver or Christmas music or, heaven help me, the Doodletown Pipers. I may have been thinking about the opera, the power of a single note. About how one note in a performance can be disastrous; even a faltering crack in the voice can tear a hole in self-esteem. If the mistake is repeated, a second, third, or fourth time, the hole becomes large enough to swallow the beauty in the song, the interpretation of the singer. Composure is a funny thing. If it is lost completely, maybe even just once, there is no telling how one might regroup, start again . . .

. . . waiting for the test results . . .

. . . the power of just one single note, one single moment. Like the high A I hit in Puccini's *Suor Angelica*, the way I was caught up in the purity of that last note, time suspended, and the oneness I felt with the nun, the one who felt the separation from forgiveness, from hope, from her illegitimate baby.

Probably I was thinking nothing at all, simply trying to hold the fear, the guilt at bay.

She wore white, like a nurse, this black woman facing me. The test was positive, she said. "Do you want to terminate it?" she finally got around to asking.

"No," I said. I was stunned and confused, but this much I knew, never once questioned: this baby was to be mine.

This was me, always Miss Clean and Perfect in the eyes of others, the one who worked hard on appearances with an aptitude for work and mercy: part performer, part teacher, part nun. I was pregnant and not married. Certainly not sinless, but never *this* stained. What is it about sexual sin? What drives it so deep, so hard that decades later it is as scarlet—the shade of red in blood—as the day it was birthed? What about it calls up lame excuses and rationalizations, wild and unconnected lies, when all is said and done, in the hope that nothing had ever been said or done? Why is it different from cheating on an exam or serving time or cursing your neighbor? What makes it so immune to feeling forgiven, by God and by others? What is it that so easily rebukes redemption, grace?

I had no one but myself to blame. Losing my virginity was a conscious choice. There was no peer pressure, no twisting of my arm, no justifiable excuse. I simply wanted to lose myself in Ernest, to formalize in the most intimate way the love and commitment that he and I shared. Desire overwhelmed reason and regret. We were careful, protected, and prepared; we were safe, we thought.

But sin is never safe, and when it comes to sex, sin packs an appetite for destruction. The consequences fell smoking and to this day still burn inside me. *What would be the damage?* I wondered as I left the clinic that day. *How could I handle this kind of failure? Wasn't it just a few months earlier that I had been rejected at the Curtis Institute of Music? I had just begun to put myself back together, to feel an edge of respect, and now this. Would Ernest reject me too? And what about my parents and God?*

Ernest, over the phone, was cool, puzzled, and finally rational. "Well, how did that happen?" he asked at first. I was silent, familiar as he with Biology 101, and waited for any inflection, twist of a word, hesitation, anything at all that would hint of abandonment. "Things like that happen," he said recovering. "I'm coming home next weekend. We'll drive up and talk to my parents and then we'll talk to yours." It was a no-hem-haw, take-charge, I-will-take-full-responsibility tone of voice—the very reason I so easily gave myself to him so completely in trust. We were going to get on with it. Together.

My daddy simply said, "Okay, big daughter," with a look that said. "We love you, no matter what." My mother sighed. Not a sigh of disgust, but simply an acknowledgment of the inevitable disruption of my life. Ernest's parents were naturally disappointed but also supportive. Both sets of parents gave us money and furniture—solid things, expressions of love we could build on.

I decided to drop out of school. This needed to be as much of an ending as it was a beginning. We told no one except our parents and my husband's best man. Not even the preacher who married us on January 4, 1972, at Stewart Air Force Base knew. It was our protected secret.

A storm of opposing emotions raged in me. Inside me was growing a thing of beauty—fingers, toes, heart—flesh of our flesh, our baby, the anticipation of overwhelming joy. At the same time I was often immersed in feelings of doubt, fear, and guilt. I was fueled by anger, not at Ernest or the baby; I was upset with myself. The friction between the joy and my anger at myself generated energy, which I somehow redirected. I got busy, impregnated with the details of life.

We had to move on. The quicker the better.

76

In the numbing blitz of emotion I didn't know that I would move on, yet feel stuck. It was a harrowing transition, as poorly conceived as a novel by someone named Emily Dickens. No one could have been fooled into thinking the first year of our marriage was poetry.

We moved from Ohio to West Point, New York, where Ernest worked as first lieutenant, general staff. I had lost a great deal in the move—connections with art, community, purpose, self-esteem—but I had not lost my naïveté. I believed, as I always had, that with enough work, enough sacrifice, enough prayer, enough of whatever was required from me, things would work out with minimal tension. After all, I was in love with a man whom I knew to be strong, if not faultless; he stood by me, filled me, caressed me, taught me, moved me, loved me. I was soon to have a baby, who was very much wanted and already loved. What were the sacrifices compared to those kinds of connections? Even if I had to give up what I once believed were deep parts of me, I knew that I was loved and that I would love.

Ernest and I set up home in an apartment at Stewart Air Force Base, which was a forty-five-minute drive from West Point. The apartment had an upstairs, downstairs, and two bedrooms. In addition to the household goods our relatives and friends had given us, we had to rent furniture. The first two weeks were busy with choosing, unpacking, situating, shutting out the dead of winter. We did rather well. I was prepared to do whatever was necessary.

What I wasn't prepared for was our first fight. In the two years that we were dating and engaged, Ernest and I never had had a cross word with one another. People who never spar make two-bit fighters. Two weeks after we were married, Ernest came home and said, "What have *you* been doing all day?" I understood in a flash the heart that beats in a crime of passion. I felt fire in places that I never knew even existed in me; I tried to burn a stare into him. I felt reduced, like the multiplication of a fraction, to the lowest common denominator. But that wasn't the worst of it. I was, in my feeling like a zero, doing nothing to stand up for myself. I figured that somehow this must be my fault. There was no one to blame but me.

That is when I felt the icy fingers of a New York winter, the chill that falls even between lovers. I felt isolated, stripped like the black threads of a tree in February. I had no recourse. I had left my friends, my art, my plans—the pieces of a dream—in Cincinnati for this: the expected regiment of dustless wood and steel and glass, the precise mercy of someone else's expectations, the cool flesh of someone else's dream. I could not drive; I had no friends yet; I was disconnected from my family; I was alone with my expanding womb and words underscored with accusation: *What have* you *been doing?* With marriage, especially considering our circumstances, I expected some sacrifices. I was surprised and frightened to feel so much like a martyr.

From my perspective, Ernest had it all: prestige, status, respect, dignity, presence of command, *and* family. I had Ernest. That was it, both a common expectation and a root of bitterness. Stripped of an environment that had sparked and nurtured me, I felt the want of an identity. I possessed only the identity that Ernest was able or willing to spare. That arrangement, of course, was unfair to both of us.

We both could have handled things better. I should have realized that my identity does not lie in what I *do* but in who I *am*. I simply wasn't spiritual enough and fought against words that had the easy ring of jargon. Ernest was busy and captive to presuppositions; he had neither the time nor the pull of conscience to change immediately.

The first year of our marriage, then, was both challenging and vital. In a way our isolation served us well; we were left to ourselves to deal with our problems and misunderstandings. We were not left with the option of ignoring our difficulty, as if we could tolerate a lion in the kitchen as merely an unpleasant surprise: we would either deal with it or get eaten alive. No choice, in the end.

That is not to say that I didn't retreat into my music, the remnant of it, and the seed of hope that was sprouting deep within me. This was not just a pregnancy. This was our child. I would play hymns at the piano, finding the refuge of my mother, and hope they would sink in to the place of kicks and heartbeats. I knew that I could reach our child with music, with words, with unspoken acceptance, even in the darkness, the womb-like isolation. More than a cord tied us together. I would take walks and talk to our baby: describe the beauty out here, describe what I am like, what Ernest is like. I would talk of the love we shared and the love we hoped to develop. In the evening or when the baby fussed, I would place headphones on my swollen abdomen and play Brahms or Rachmaninoff, like the waves in a womb, the calming of a troubled sea.

Storms raged outside my womb too: Ernest and I, both selfish, both frightened in our separate ways by the guttural rumbling of change, longed for a deeper faith. At first all I wanted was peace, at all costs. If I didn't blame myself, I would at the very least not blame Ernest. I was afraid of the anger inside, deeper even than our baby, and the ugliness that anger stirred. Ernest is an intelligent man; he knew that I would sweep points of tension inside rather than away. For the sake of not wanting to feel the hunger of stress, I would usually eat my point of view.

I would explode in little bits and pieces, with sharp questions, elsewhere. I had joined a women's Bible study on the base and led a choir at church. I wanted in part for my faith and music to keep me busy, to prevent me from sinking down into the tension. Ernest also was deepening his faith, partly as a reaction, a stronghold against the discord. Beyond that, we both hungered for God, and that over time is what transformed our desires, our marriage.

But transformation—the kind of heat necessary to melt stone hearts—is never passive. Sin does not die of natural causes; it needs to be killed. For Ernest and me, the situation was complicated by our understanding (or lack of) of the roles in marriage: husband, wife, submission. The husband, in this case an officer, was in charge; the wife, if she was godly, was expected, for her own good, to develop a salute of respect. Spit polished, perfectly creased, lines defined: these were the molds that we understood and wanted desperately to shape our lives around, for the sake of tradition or maybe convenience.

The women's Bible study explored the role women should play. Again I heard: *obedience, submission, weaker vessel, helpmate.* I tried. I dusted more, tried new recipes, held my tongue, and nearly suffocated in the dustless, antiseptic smell of the silence. Even I, the one given to pleasing others, suspected something was wrong, out of kilter. One particular Bible study pushed me over the edge: Sarah, it was concluded, was obedient in spirit to Abraham by permitting him to lie. Submission, it seemed, was more important than a respect for truth. Finally I spoke what was on my mind. At the end of one of the next studies, I asked the nearly unspeakable questions: "Doesn't anyone else besides me feel like a second-class citizen? Is it possible that we have poorly interpreted what submission means? Sometimes I feel squelched, trapped. Why am I feeling these things?" The dam broke. For the next two hours, these women talked about how we had all felt those same feelings, and without anger we admitted our frustrations. Such honesty was cleansing.

My concerns were amplified by the past, present, and future. Why had God given me talent and training to do certain things if he intended for me only to clean house? And why, in my growing confusion, did I feel so trapped, useless, abandoned to a mold that did not encompass all of who I was? And why, in God's name, was I permitted so few dreams of my own? For the next few years I wrestled with such questions, sorting out biblical truth and religious culture. The process involved not only a stripping away of preconceived notions but also my constant need to appear righteous in the eyes of others: the constant doing-saying-thinking the way I thought others desired. Gradually, I became more interested in discovering who God created me to be rather than fashioning myself around what I interpreted others wanted me to be.

I wrestled at first without Ernest. When I shared my concerns about identity and male-female roles with him, he often interpreted those feelings as a dissatisfaction with him, which wasn't the case. For the sake of peace, I churned alone. At this point, Ernest simply couldn't hear what I was trying to say. It was only years later that the same issues resurfaced between the two of us.

Despite the tension and lack of communication in the early years of our marriage, Ernest and I continued to share good times. Our love, although sometimes disturbed, was never questioned; we were committed to each other, and that often surfaced with joy. In the middle of nowhere, on a still lake, I remember the rainbow trout that we caught, the way the color would catch in our laughter. I remember the feeling I had at the chaperoned parties for the cadets, the flashed salutes, the stirring of respect and pride for my husband. Or the nights in the summer heat, I remember the way our bodies would melt into each other, all the way to one soul.

And then there was Martin, our firstborn. He was always with us, in the womb at first, a living, growing reminder of the love we shared. The joy of his coming we welcomed; the guilt we managed or submerged. I could only anticipate the love that we would share, mother and child and father. Martin took us by surprise. On the afternoon of July 26, 1972, I had some pains; it felt like indigestion. Our baby was not due until the end of August, and I had had some bleeding and pain already, so I walked off the pain. The cycle repeated itself—pain-walk-okay—five or six times; it never crossed my mind that I was in labor. At two o'clock in the morning, I woke up in pain and called the hospital. They didn't think it was anything; they told me to take it easy.

Finally, seated on the toilet and doubled over in pain, I woke Ernest and asked him to take me to the hospital. Ernest, always in command, was in a fog, awakened from sleep to the pending arrival of our first child, "Huh, huh?" I was cool as a cucumber, ticking off a list of things that needed to be done. Ernest and I had taken Lamaze training together, but I was beginning to think that he was the one who needed the breathing exercises. He would stay with me, he promised, until they took me to the delivery room. The idea of blood kept him from swearing further oaths.

We got to the hospital an hour later, and the medical staff measured the width of my dilation. Just as the nurse was saying that I was fully dilated, Ernest walked into the room, decked out in a hospital gown and mask. "Where are you going?" I asked him.

"Into the delivery room," he said as if he had never given it a second thought. I could tell, even in my pain, that he was fidgety, excited, and in very unfamiliar territory. As I was being wheeled into the delivery room, the nurse kept banging my bed into the door, not once but repeatedly. Ernest told the nurse to step aside and wheeled me into the delivery room himself. Eight contractions and a few minutes later, our firstborn had arrived: his eyes open; jet black, shiny curls; a cute cap; a touch that set off an instant smile. The two made one, love made flesh and bone.

The next four years were marked by change, both slow and fast. We moved three times—from West Point to Germany to Boston to Cleveland. In the same period, Ernest went from officer to private sector to boss. In the swirl of motion, my life was mostly the same; change came steadily, without flash, soft colors in a steady monotony, like music drawn by the marking of a metronome. I was, in a mostly good sense, doing time.

We moved to Germany two months after Martin was born. I had hoped for intrigue. Instead I became immersed in caring for our infant son and a kind of love that washed me clean, bright, new, even in the dirtiest and dullest of moments. I was stunned by watching him sleep.

Ernest worked in Frankfurt, about three hours from where we lived in Baumholder. He came home only on weekends. Our relationship matured, as much as circumstances would allow, and I remember the roller coaster of weekdays-weekend: anticipation, enjoyment, sadness, life goes on. I did part-time volunteer work as a dental assistant, directed the church choir, jogged with Ernest, attended the opera, gave a recital, made baby food, and learned to make friends. I was growing as a Christian. I attended Bible studies, discovered more who I was, channeled my creativity into my family, and felt more comfortable.

Within a year we moved back to the States and rented the downstairs of a home from a man who claimed he would never rent to anyone who had children. Our family and his became close. Ernest took a job as a cost engineer with one of the largest construction companies in the United States. In October 1974, the company transferred him to Cleveland, where he was cost engineer, assistant superintendent, value engineer, and project engineer.

I was happy to move to Cleveland; we were both closer to our families. Following the movement of our lives in the last few years, I longed for roots, for stability, for more of the touch of certainty.

In many ways I felt that during the first few years of our marriage, we had simply wandered in a wasteland. At the time I could see no value in these times. Yet in looking back, I have been able to evaluate more clearly the purpose in the desert. What I saw as wasted time—the inability to use my formal training and schooled gifts—was actually deepening me, forcing me to drive my roots to deeper levels for nourishment. In this desert I learned to deal with ordinary life. Not every day is a Sunday or a center-stage spotlight or applause or excellent grades. In this nonstorybook life I faced lessons far more difficult than those I had faced in college. Through the discipline of the everyday, the mundane, the disappointments and failures, I began to develop balance and build spiritual muscle that could grapple with reality.

Even the sin and guilt marked me, in a strange way, for grace. I certainly have felt the soul-deep pain of sin's rent—and I still fight the urge to gloss it over in denial—yet through it all I have begun to recognize what it means to be ransomed by grace. That has made me, at the same time, more comfortable and disquieted with myself. The great gifts of grace, I believe, are these: forgiveness of what has passed and longing for what might yet be. Such is the thorned and rosy path of holiness.

I have debated the wisdom of such self-revelation. Should I hide the sin that has been, and still is, in my life? Will such stories seem to blot out God's goodness, to invalidate the positive that he has been able to perform in and through me? I don't think so. I have come to believe that my sin and mistakes, while worthy of the fires of hell, magnify God's great arrangement of grace. The miracles of God's sovereignty are always this: he still chooses to work through each of us. Sin that is scarlet, through the arc of the cross, is bloodwashed white as snow.

Christians, the real heroes of faith, shine in spite of themselves. The people whom I have looked up to the most are not the ones who seem perfect and untouched but rather those whose wounds, while healed, have left battle scars. Jesus Christ knows this: sin leaves its marks; even he, with the scars through eternity, does not attempt to hide that fact. The scars of sin speak of this: we have been healed, but we are not left unmarked by the stain of such sin or, even more, by the stubbornness of such grace. The sins in each of our lives should teach us that we are human, each prone to selfishness, yet capable through grace of doing the very will of God himself.

In my own life, I think, I have spent too much time trying to hide my scars, believing that once they were exposed, others would hold me accountable, coin me unredeemable, prey on my weakness, discredit my walk with God, and banish me from the community. Yet I have found that through the very act of peeling back the veil and sharing the bittersweet in my life, I have less to fear. Sin can control us by keeping us in hiding. Through the vulnerability of showing our scars, we can loose its secret grip, encourage one another to fight on, and visibly convict the community of God that sin is always a wound. It is then, in our shared healing and love, that we can move on.

To move on. That is, even in our spiritual immaturity, the lesson that Ernest and I learned through those difficult, early years of marriage. We learned to forget what was behind and to press forward, always remembering that movement brings constant change.

When we moved to Cleveland in October of 1974, finally

dropping some roots, we were wiser, more mature, with deeper love—for each other and for God. The wasteland of the years just passed, without our really knowing it, had in some mysterious ways caused each of us to blossom.

Yet despite the purposeful act of settling in, the transitions were no less harrowing. Ernest wrestled with his work; often he found himself asked to cross ethical lines, which he finally could not do. After moving to Cleveland, he took three jobs within ten years before starting his own business.

I also was struggling at times. In the summer of 1976, I had a miscarriage, one that very nearly cost me my life as well: for three months, the baby had grown in my fallopian tube. During the surgery, the doctor had asked for a camera; he had never before seen anything so large in that genre of tube. I had lost so much blood that the doctor had leaned over and told me, "Young lady, somebody must be looking out for you."

It took a while for the miscarriage to shake me. Six weeks after the surgery, I returned to the doctor for a checkup. In the waiting room, I saw babies in their mother's arms, and my loss hit me. I fought back a wave of tears, my empty arms crossed. Still the sense of emptiness went deeper than that. It was more than the stark fact that I had only a fifty-fifty chance of getting pregnant again. It was more than an empty crib. It was this: I wondered what was next. Before the miscarriage, I had sensed a slow and almost unnoticed progression in my life: my spiritual life was deepening; I was much less defensive and confused; I felt anchored in the Lord and in my growing relationships with Ernest and Martin; I was teaching piano, directing choir, and using my spiritual gifts. The child that I carried, in some sense, seemed like a metaphor for the growth in my life. Now the child, without a name, without me even being able to find out its sex, was gone, cut from me.

Beyond my womb, I felt the emptiness.

What next?

*D*ebbie would have loved the '60s. She was hard, petite, rebellious. I got to know Debbie as she visited her husband, who was in the hospital with cancer.

In a way we were bookends, reverse images of one another. I was innocent, naive, and protected; she was wild, street-wise, and hammered hard like a nail. Debbie would often confide nasty moments of hers, trying to get a rise out of me. We were, in some unusual manner, drawn to each other.

I gave her the keys to my office (she refused to leave her husband), and my family and I even took her to a jazz concert once. Hoping to reach her, I crossed all professional boundaries.

But just when I thought I was breaking through, making an impact on her, she became suicidal. I met with Debbie's psychiatrist and the social worker, both of whom advised me to break off the relationship. It was a valuable lesson. Since then, I have learned to see the difference between people who need just a little more and people who seem to never get enough. What creates that difference? God only knows.

Chapter Five

Music and the Mentally Retarded: Therapy of the Soul

Maestoso (dignified)

Introduction to Music Therapy. The title of the course caught my eye. It was the combination of the words *music* and *therapy*, with the unexpected and unsettling juxtaposition of, say, *river* and *hope*, that rushed in a deep part of me, surprised me with its flood of possibility.

In the fall of 1976, a few months after my miscarriage, I had enrolled at Cleveland State University to complete my master's degree in voice. I was unsure of what I wanted to do, but I felt the need to do something. During the spring semester of 1977, I saw the course title: Introduction to Music Therapy. Something stole along subconscious synapses, washing me in an electrical bath of memories: college years, the broken dreams of music, and childhood, of wanting and always striving to heal. Music and therapy. Was it possible? Could it bridge the unmeasured chasms between art and science, performance and technique, steely law and mushy grace? Could it connect the desires of my heart?

In those days, music therapy was still in its infancy, little more than a birthed theory. The profession started in 1950, as it was officially documented, coming in the aftershock of bombing in World War II. Caregivers noticed that when they played music in wards filled with shell-shocked soldiers, the music would have a calming effect: patients needed fewer medications, felt more peace of mind, experienced less frenzy. From there research emerged: music therapy helped to lower blood pressure and increased the body's production of certain hormones and endorphins, the body's natural pain killers; and listening to music decreased the neurotransmitters available to relay pain messages.

The art of music and the science of healing. In the fall quarter of 1977, I enrolled in the music-therapy class. I was immediately hooked. My teacher was about the size of a sixth grader, a regular red brick of an adult, studied in art and manner, businesslike. I remember that I had to have minor surgery, which was scheduled the day before a test. When I asked my teacher if I could take the test early, she snapped, "Take the test when it is given or take a zero." I had the surgery to remove a cyst from my lip on Friday night, the test Saturday morning, and a bit of teeth grinding in between. I sensed something, maybe the ring of the words, like the ding of a kindergarten triangle, that deeply: music therapy.

Of the twenty people in the class, only thirteen would be allowed to move on in the music-therapy program. At the end of the class, I was accepted. Since I already had a bachelor's degree in music, I did not have to start from scratch to obtain a degree in music therapy; I simply had to make up the differences in the two curricula, primarily classes about the specifics of music therapy. These courses were then followed by a six-month internship; the entire process of earning my degree, called a postgraduate music-therapy equivalency degree, took from September of 1976 to June of 1979.

In many ways my studies with music therapy were similar to my experience with music performance in college. Music therapy included both art and science, technique and interpretation, and just as I had done before, I was swimming in over-all moments, drowning in details. Put me in a music and special education class focused on application, and I would fly: the creative buzz in my mind stirred up remedies, activities, potential solutions, grace-filled renderings. Put me in an acoustics class, the formulaic study of the phenomena of sound, and I would suffocate in vowels and microtubules and oscillators and diction, the technical movement of tongue, lung, diaphragm, and brain. Again I felt the distinction between my heart, brain, and fingers—theory and beauty.

Study in music therapy involved studying the body—anatomy, physiology, biology—and the psyche—philosophies of behavior modification, Gestalt psychology, transactional analysis, other eclectic philosophical models. And then there was the music, of course, the heart of the program: procedures, protocols, techniques, methods. We were required, for instance, to know a broad range of music, to learn to play one instrument from each of the orchestral families: I would play the tuba one semester, the clarinet the next, the drum after that.

I excelled, less fearful than I had been in college. I had no high notes here to choke on and no pressure of performing. I didn't have the feeling of faking it, of something not quite being right.

Well into the program, each of us had to do a special project connecting theory with treatment. I chose alcoholism: How can the alcoholic be treated with music therapy? I worked from a simple model: analysis of the disease, symptomatology, the intervention of treatment. In researching the project, I visited a local alcohol rehabilitation facility and interviewed its director. When I saw the people in rehabilitation, I longed to do something for them; their need was almost palpable. I wanted to begin a music-therapy session immediately, or at least touch them, do something to help them recover a sense of dignity. But this was just a project and a research paper; I had to cool my jets.

Although I loved and excelled in my studies, music therapy still had the metallic feel of science, of unproven theory, of $x + y = z$, of doctor-patient-sickness-treatment, a high degree of disconnectedness. How else can I say it? I wasn't at all sure that the equation would fly, that the art could transcend the science, that the therapy with all its bony reason could hold up in anything so fragile as a human touch.

Then my resurrected and cemented fear taunted: *Can you do this?* In the back of my head was the jury at the Curtis Institute of Music, the way they chewed on their pencils, looked distracted, shot off their judgment: "not good enough, rejected," with the tone of voice of a sixth-grade boy announcing, "Deforia, IQ 106. What an idiot!" Even now, a competent adult, these voices haunted me.

The message—music therapy—and the messenger—me, music therapist. I wasn't sure that the *how* or the *who* would really be able to work. I soon got the chance to find out. To be certified as a music therapist, I had to complete a six-month internship. Only two music-therapy internships were available in the city of Cleveland at the time, and I was fortunate to be chosen for one of them. From January through June of 1979, under the supervision of Louise Steele, head of the Cleveland Music School Settlement, I fulfilled my internship requirements. The settlement consisted of two departments: one for music therapists and another for classical music study. I practiced concurrently at five different sites and classifications of patients: mentally retarded, geriatric, psychiatric, the behaviorally disordered, and a variety of settlement children, whose conditions ranged from blindness, psychiatrically disturbed, abused, to developmentally delayed.

There was, first of all, the sheer weight of it. This was me, lacking a sense of the gravity of things, light and naïve, a continual blossom of optimism. I suddenly was locked in a psychiatric elevator, all of us headed for a piano, arriving at the conclusion that these were people like me, only scarred in different ways. I found myself at the nursing home, with its reek of ammonia and urine, like everyone simultaneously had had a Pine-Sol bowel movement, the odor so overpowering that it could knock out my compassion, make me doubt that beauty exists anywhere, let alone on the outside of this carefully manicured façade. Or I found myself face-to-face with a profoundly retarded boy, twelve and in diapers, spitting up more oatmeal than he ate, protected from the world by a sort of crash helmet, his mind steeled in on itself.

I found other surprises, mostly in the faces of people. A nursing-home patient who had not talked for years spoke words in music, not just once, but each time I was there, to the outlandish applause of everyone. I think of Albert, in his mid-forties, black and bald, sitting in his wheelchair, incapable of speech. One day as he sat drooling, his eyes vacant, he heard the music and fought wildly to make a noise, a small one that still screams for me to hear, to know its meaning. I think of the forty-year-old woman who had children the same age as mine. She had a progressive disease that caused everything to contract and tighten, except her eyes, which danced—I mean did a jitterbug—in response to music. All the while, I was announced by a nurse's aide as the woman who was here "to do her little music thing." Such arrogance side by side such grace.

I was not frightened by anything, really: the enormity of the injustice, the power of the music, or the way some people had just shut down so that nothing, not even a pin prick or a struck chord, could break through or puncture the deflation, the sad and wrinkled face of a half-filled balloon. I saw only possibility. In the desperation or apathy of most of the people, I wanted to do something to help, to heal, to fix it for a moment. I was not so naïve that I could not content myself with bits of time; even I knew that I couldn't change their circumstances. I just wanted my little corner, some space for temporary magic. I prayed to the Lord to give me a way to help each of them see a glimpse of beauty in his or her splintered-mirror world. Just a smile or a turn of a head or a flash of a tender memory. Just a few seconds, if that is all there was to give.

Most of all I needed to prove myself. I had to overcome the nagging fear that I didn't really have anything to offer to anyone. I longed to move from theory to reality. The greater part of that transition, I remember, occurred during one particular moment. It wasn't stunning, like the unwed nun hitting a high

A, but mundane, a kind of slightly left-of-center perception that bites on a gray day. I was at the Settlement with one of my five supervisors, Ann Kent, who was attempting to show me a procedure she was using to get a six-year-old profoundly retarded boy to pick up an object. Ann would shake a tambourine, place it on her lap, then hold out her hands and say, "Give me the tambourine, Chris." Chris, eager to imitate, would also hold out his hands, totally missing the point.

As I watched the scene repeat itself, I timidly made a suggestion. "Ann, why don't you try to put the tambourine on the floor, about three feet away from you, point to it, and then ask him to pick it up?" When she did, the boy responded immediately.

I remember I felt somewhat awkward—I was the student, she was the supervisor. But instead of taking offense, she offered her appreciation. That was a beginning for me, the first kindling of the idea, *I'm good*. It was a transformation from student to therapist, from insecure child to confident adult. It was such a little thing, but that moment was a turning point in my life, a beginning.

During the six months of the internship, the Lord blessed me with a series of minor miracles. Brian was the first. When he arrived, he was two and a half years old, the youngest child ever to come to the Settlement. He was developmentally disabled, could not speak any words, and hyperactive; at best, he could not sit still for more than two minutes. The doctors had suggested a heavy diet of stimulation.

Because I was a mother, they let me work with Brian. I started with simple cause and effect. First, I would bang a drum, and as I hit it, I would say, "Hit." Then I would put his hand over mine and do the same thing. I also did a lot of massaging of his arms and hands, putting his hand up to my throat to feel the vibration of the word *hit*. Brian began to make a certain sound. Then I used a drum and maraca and sang, "Boom, boom, boom goes the big bass drum!" and in a softer and higher pitch, "Shake, shake, shake goes the maraca." Soon he was able to differentiate between the words; he knew their meanings.

My songs were very monotonous, the same tones, day

after day. "This is a drum," I was singing one day. "This is a drum. This is a drum." And in the middle of the repetition, "This is," Brian said, "drum," out of the blue. It was his first word. As he said it, I heard something like a chair fall. On the other side of a one-way mirror, his mother was stunned: her little boy had spoken for the first time, with purpose. A few days later he spoke spontaneously. Later he asked for one of the instruments by name.

Then there was Tammy Christmas, no kidding. She was eight years old, blind, and talkative. When I tried to converse with her, she would interrupt in a rapid-fire voice at least fifteen times a minute. She talked nonstop: when she played the piano, sat, stood, walked, breathed. My first goal was to get Tammy to listen. She loved the piano, so I would say to her, "If you can listen for thirty seconds without interrupting, I will teach you to play a song, or I will give you the biggest hug you ever had." So we'd try. I could see her holding back her words, as if they were trained seals, disciplined to the point of being ready to burst. But she would make it. "Yes!" I would cheer, "You made it." Over time she began to settle.

Tammy Christmas had a gift for music. After her mother would take her to a choir rehearsal, she could play the pieces on the piano. She had an excellent auditory memory and dreamed of a future in music. But when it came to more complex pieces of music, she couldn't learn all the notes by ear. She would be limited in her music until she could somehow learn to read music.

I tried, it seemed, a hundred different options. Even though she was legally blind, she could see just a little. I attempted to write large and dark notes, nearly the size of letters above a chalkboard, but it took forever to score "When the Saints Come Marching In," let alone Mozart. I researched musical braille but learned it was far too complex for an eight-year-old. So I did it hodgepodge, making it up as we went. She learned rhythm—the pace of whole notes, half notes, quarter notes, etc.—and how to play on other instruments, like drums and handbells. In addition to learning the music, Tammy also

93

had to learn behavioral skills: to remain focused, to sit still and not rock, to slow her mind and body. Eventually she was interrupting me only two or three times every forty-five minutes.

By the end of the six months, through a cooked-up recipe, Tammy was ready for a recital. Tammy, true to her name, was dressed up like a Christmas tree. She walked up, introduced her piece, sat, sang and played a song about a chicken and egg:

> Oh, I had a little chicken, and she wouldn't lay an egg.
> So I poured hot water up and down her leg.
> And she wiggled and she wobbled and she shook her little head;
> Then the poor little chicken laid a hard-boiled egg.

Beyond the audience's laughter was a sense of amazement. Here was the little blind girl who had not been able to stay quiet, performing in front of an audience, taking a bow, lit up, red and green in spirit.

Having a visible impact and using my God-given abilities and training to change lives was new to me. Earlier in my life I had been a part-time clerk at Strawbridge & Clothier, a worker in the school cafeteria, a woman who loved her family, but all the while I felt slightly wasted, as if I could do more if I could get over my inadequacy. I know it sounds strange: I wanted to give of myself, genuinely, partly for selfish reasons.

Near the end of my internship in the summer of 1979, I was attending an evening board meeting at the building that housed the handicapped children with whom I was working. During the meeting I noticed that a representative from the Cuyahoga County Board of Mental Retardation, Dottie Joyce, was sitting beside me. I took my pen and wrote on a napkin, "Do you know anybody who needs an energetic music therapist?"

She wrote back, "Call me at my office tomorrow." I think my eyes bulged. As it turned out, a music teacher was getting married, leaving a position open in the fall.

Before my meeting with the county's director of personnel, I decided to go to the school, called Raub Developmental Center, which had a forty-person staff that worked with more than two hundred mentally handicapped children with IQs of 50 and below. On this particular day, the developmental center was having a program with all the children present. What I saw in that gymnasium was unlike anything else I had ever seen: the full range of humanity, from profoundly and severely retarded to disfigured. Most obvious was the noise and smell, a crossfire of senses, a blur of motion. Class by class, they took the stage, a maze of different configurations: children rocking, buzzing, drooling into towels, hugging, grunting, wearing helmets, absent in the world, present with pride. Some were, in the jargon, highly functioning, capable of carrying a tune or a toothy smile. Others were totally dependent, trapped in themselves, racing inside. Mostly they were busy, riding a purpose. Each child had been given something to do, even if he or she could do nothing. Those who could, would sing or play or read. Those who couldn't, would ride in wheelchairs decorated with flags, parading, in the best sense of the word, their stuff, their essential stuff.

Where many people would see only chaos, the overall brokenness of it, I saw an opportunity. My mind, stormed by my senses, cracked and flowed, burst with possibilities: I could do this and that and this and that. I mean, really, I could *do* these things. I knew it, beyond my five senses, knew it in whatever sticks in the heart.

The next day in the personnel director's office, I must have seemed slightly beside myself, almost like a child at Christmas. To say that I was enthusiastic would be to say that Santa Claus was jolly. The director asked me if I knew what all of this was about, and I ripped into a zealous description of my observations at Raub, feeling uncommonly bold and sincere, rattling off procedures, techniques, instruments, what I would do and use, my theories on touch, therapy, heart connections, all in one sentence, not surfacing, not even once, for a breath.

I must have sounded crazy. Like someone shell-shocked, he looked at me and said, "Young lady, you've got the job."

I said, "But you don't even know me."

He said, in effect, "You have affected me and soon you will

affect others." He knew it as I knew it, deep down, where assurance is different from pride. I was dignified, chit-chatted as if I seriously meant it, left, got in the elevator, pushed a button, waited to start dropping, and screamed! I did a little dance, like a bowler after a strike, and *screamed*! We're talking primal, all the way back to Jacob's angel screaming *uncle*, the in-your-face joy, the transforming kind. I had landed a job, which I was to begin in September. My first real job!

"YES!" That was it, in one long guttural syllable.

Seizure. Doctors describe it as an electrical storm: unorganized, uncontrolled, and unimaginably violent. It starts mysteriously in deep recesses of the brain, breeding on some unknown cue, spreading impulses like fire through neurons. Muscles contract, bowels move, energy is devoured. For a few seconds, sometimes up to a minute, the body is usually locked in the fetal position. Afterward the victim has temporary memory loss and lies in a dreamlike state.

When one of the students at Raub suffered a seizure, the teacher would dutifully write it down on a chart or click a counter on the belt, timing its duration, or, on a good day, joke about the pee on the carpet. No big deal.

All, somehow, for God's glory. I don't profess to be much of a theologian, have never, up to now, used the word *hypostasis*, although I read the Bible daily. A few verses in John trouble me. Here is the situation detailed in the first three verses of John 9: While traveling, Jesus sees a blind man; his disciples ask whose sin was responsible for the blind man's condition. A good question. Jesus replies, in his enigmatic fashion, that no one's sin was responsible. So far so good. But then Jesus goes on to a startling and perplexing conclusion: this man's blindness happened so that the work of God might be displayed in his life.

What could this mean? That God allows suffering for his glory? That God will heal everyone who suffers? And what about the children, like Eric, autistic and agitated, who in the few years that I knew him never let anyone or anything break through, except the constant fingering of his own mouth? Eric would grow from young and broken to old and broken, and along the way express only sadness or violence. What about Eric?

And what about the parents of children like Eric, once filled with hope and energy and drive? What about the parents who grow old too, quicker than most, and in their weariness, their bone fatigue, gloss over, break up, shut down?

For what, God's glory? I'm not going to answer that in full, because experience, if nothing else, has taught me we can never know in full. We gaze through a glass darkly. I have chosen not to wrestle with the *why* question. God is God and suffering is suffering, and what I think is not going to change either God or the suffering. He and it will still be there. I have tried, instead, to focus on answers, if not really answers, then openings.

With almost all the children I worked with at Raub, no matter how profoundly retarded or alone, I usually found some opening, some rip in the curtain that separates them from the rest of the world, that traps them in a broken body. I kept looking for it, praying for grace, finally spotting the tear through which we could give to each other something beautiful: a song, a few notes, a laugh. The break may be tiny, open only for a flash, and then gone, sometimes forever. But the opportunity, nonetheless was there, for connection, for touch, for God's grace in an otherwise graceless life—a transforming and transformed moment.

Part of what Christ's response to his disciples in John 9 means, I believe, is that God wants us to be lovers. For it is through us, his people, that God displays his work, which is his transforming love. Suffering, in all its strangeness, allows us special opportunities to demonstrate God's love to those who feel unloved and broken.

Something else strikes me. The most profoundly retarded children at Raub taught me the most. Sometimes their behavior was almost subhuman, life at its most base: drooling, eating, gagging, spitting up, peeing, fighting, clenching, sleeping. Yet at times they would arrest me with something distinctly human, a dim sparkle of soul that made me stop and take inventory. Looking for the smallest responses makes a person realize what is large in life: a touch, a smile, a gift. It is, I know, a big price for these children to pay, but it is nonetheless a measure of value.

I don't mean to make this sound glorious or distorted. It was anything but glorious, what with the routine and the smell of poop, and if the truth be known, most of the children at the school found the opening in me before I could do a thing for them, passing out slobbery kisses as if they were cherry lollipops. Many of the children were only mildly retarded, didn't drool or moan, and could love you at the drop of a hat. Without the adult crust of fear, they were able to give in openness and trust, unconditionally. Others, mildly or profoundly retarded, were mean-spirited or wallflowers or ego-centered. In other words, they all fell somewhere on the human scale, just like the rest of us.

And just like the rest of us, they wanted to express themselves, to be understood and heard, to make connections. I tried to get in each child's world, look out from his or her eyes, and know the barriers that kept him or her at a distance. Music, of course, was my primary tool. Even the most profoundly retarded child can respond to sound, movement, or vibration. Something in music has the ability to move, to elicit feeling, even, and maybe especially, in the most desperate of situations. I knew that in theory. Within the first year at Raub, mainly through working with three students—Joey, Scott, and Sherri—I would come to know the power of music in reality.

Joey, a seven-year-old with cocker spaniel eyes, had shut down. He had spoken when he was younger, but a virus or some other trauma had caused him to stop; he was operating on a three- or four-year-old level and was labeled developmentally delayed. He sang his name, "Jo-ey," and that was the extent of his language skills. The first time I saw Joey, I melted: long black hair, small, dressed well with matching shirt and sweater, always fidgeting or moving something, maybe to keep up with his mind. In any case, I always felt there was something going on behind his eyes, in places he kept secret. Although he was nearly always agitated, bent in nervous energy, he was also passive; he would allow you to walk him from place to place without resistance.

His teacher, knowing that the only word he spoke, he sang, brought him to me. "Jo-ey," he sang, as if to remind himself, or maybe the world, that he was still here. I surrounded him with instruments; he sat in front of me. Into a toilet tissue tube, I sang, "Jo-ey."

Then I put the tube to his mouth. He sang, "Jo-ey."

I returned the tube to my mouth, choosing another similar two-syllable word, "Cook-ie."

I returned the tube to his mouth. "Cook-ie," he sang.

Then slowly after several tries, I eased the tube from his mouth and sang into the open air, "Hel-lo."

He returned, in his best singing voice, "Hel-lo."

I was astounded. Within a period of twenty minutes, we were conversing in a sing-song, echo fashion. When the teacher returned, she couldn't believe it. This child, who had only sung one word, was now learning a vocabulary.

We progressed to singing names of instruments and tools: drum, bell, fork, spoon. He soon made connections between the words and objects, catching the symbolism, understanding language. He left within a year, and I lost track of Joey, except for that special place he warmed in my heart.

Unlike Joey, Scott was not cute. He was also seven, with dark stubs for teeth, globs of black wax in his ears, a nearly constant nasal drip. Scott, tending toward autism, became agitated when anything came in close contact with his face; a tissue may have felt like sandpaper to him. In nervous energy, he made a string of percolator sounds, jumping up and down, flapping his hands to the tones he made. When he was excited, his voice would rise in volume and tone to a high-pitched scream. He hated touch, especially around his face, and went berserk when anyone tried to clean his teeth or ears. He ate only pureed food because he could not tolerate any texture in his mouth.

Scott always had a wrinkled brow, a pained expression, the look of a boy with a constant migraine. He spent most of his time trying to protect himself. It was almost as if he viewed everyone as a thief, trying to steal inside him and take something valuable. A touch was a threat, a fire, a cut. He would rather retreat than be invaded; so that is what he did.

When I started to work with Scott, I tried rocking back and forth, hoping that he would imitate me and settle, which he did. I placed a cowboy hat between us, placing my hands on his (his hands and knees were the only places he would allow me to touch), on the hat. I sang, "I've got a hat. Scott's got a hat. Oh, I've got a hat." Then, I would place the hat on my head. We did that about ten or fifteen times. After that, I repeated the same routine, but this time substituting, "Oh, *Scott's* got a hat," for, "I've got a hat." At the end of each refrain, I would place the hat slightly over his head and then worked the hat closer and closer to his head with each new repetition. Gradually I touched his head, only for a second, and then took off the hat. The next time I left it on for two seconds, then three. Whenever I saw him getting nervous, percolator sounds rising, I immediately took off the hat.

Eventually, over a six-week period, Scott wore a hat from the time he came to see me to the time he went back to his classroom! From there, we went on to a baseball cap, which came down farther over his head. I then tried the same technique to desensitize his mouth. "I've got a kazoo. I've got a kazoo. Oh, Scott's got a kazoo." Over and over and over again. Soon he would hold the kazoo in his mouth and blow it on cue.

But Scott let me go only so far. His parents still had to hold him down to clean his ears or teeth while Scott screamed, panicked, and writhed. He had, it seemed, too much at stake, too much to protect.

Sherri, also seven, wore diapers over her chunky, almost muscular body. She was black, with black hair, strong breath, and drooling expressions. She moved slowly and mechanically, unsure of her balance, looking someplace else. When I touched her hands, they would always feel wet, stiff, and contracted. She made guttural sounds when she walked and rocked back and forth when she didn't. She did not talk.

Sherri was responsive to music. Knowing that her teacher and parents desperately wanted her to be potty trained, I developed a procedure using music to help her use the toilet. I noticed that when she heard music, she would focus and settle down. After much wrestling in my mind, I came up with the idea of rigging a portable toilet that would play music. After sitting on the potty for a long time, Sherri finally peed and activated the music. When she heard the potty play "Mary Had a Little Lamb," she realized she had caused it to start. She was enthralled. Her hands stopped wringing. Eventually she learned not only to go in the potty but also to pee slowly, so that she could make the music last longer. In her trickled pee, there was an undeniable movement of grace.

A transforming moment, the break in a veil, seldom affects only one person; it often touches others as well. That is one reason I wanted to start a project that would musically intermix some of the Raub Center's children with nonhandicapped children. Whether out of ignorance, fear, or both, children often react cruelly to mentally retarded people. Through music, I thought I could bring them together, break barriers, create role models.

Before I started the project in the spring of 1980, I went to the teachers of the nursery school that I hoped would work with us. I met with parents and children. I was afraid of rejection. I explained to them that their children had been selected to be part of an innovative program meant to bridge differences. I showed them pictures of some of the Raub Center's students so that they could see that they weren't monsters who would wreak havoc on their children. I said that the Raub children selected for the program (from the higher IQ range) were, for the most part, just children too; they liked hotdogs and playing ball, but they couldn't talk or run very well. After I finished, one little boy said, "Bring them on over."

The program, called music mainstreaming, was to last six weeks. The first day was tense. Each child was quiet, watching. I said, with a lump in my throat, "Okay, everybody come sit in a circle." Then I asked them to grab a partner, which was my first mistake. The students from the nursery school grabbed each other, leaving the Raub Center children alone.

I soon learned other ways to select partners so that each nursery-school child was paired to a Raub Center child. It got better, much better. All the children wanted to play instruments, so they took turns with their partners, even if their partner happened to have stubby fingers, slanty eyes, and a thick tongue. The teachers also learned. When a child throws a maraca at your head, you definitely don't say, "Oh, the poor little retarded child." You say, "No!" At first I took ten of the developmental center's children with me, then fifteen, then twenty-one.

When the program was over, none of the children or teachers wanted it to end. We had an end-of-six-weeks party with the children. I asked the children what they liked about this experience. With many of the Raub children, who could not talk, I would have to ask yes or no questions. For example, "Did you like the music?" When I got to the nursery students, I asked them what they liked. The answers started coming, "I liked the parachute we played with," or "I liked the instruments," or "I liked the tag game." I was feeling a bit disappointed until one boy said, "I liked my new friends."

The program exploded. Other classes wanted to be involved. The local newspaper and television station did stories. In 1981, a year after we started, I got a grant from the Martha Holden Jennings Foundation to expand the program, and in 1983 the county mandated that all developmental centers have similar programs of music mainstreaming.

Shortly after starting my work at Raub Center, I started a sing-and-sign choir, which grew to twenty-five students, ranging from age fifteen to twenty-one. Many had Down's syndrome, with unintelligible speech. Some had gorgeous voices; others would make Bob Dylan sound like Pavarotti. We dressed in robes (bought for a dollar apiece from my church), learned top-ten tunes, practiced two or three times a week, and took our show on the road, to nursing homes and even to high schools. We didn't sound great. If we didn't have six or seven people who could carry a tune, it would have been hard to tell the difference between "Country Roads" and "Amazing Grace." But that wasn't the point. It was this: when the choir members had finished, they would bow, all at the same time, the synchronized movement of dignity, acceptance, and purpose, to the applause of others.

Over the years I especially remember the nursing-home visits. The speech therapist, Chris Alesnik, and I would present a full program of songs like "You Light Up My Life" and "Like a Rhinestone Cowboy," then, with the physical education specialist, Martha Trapp, we would square dance, one wheelchair resident, old and frail, and a student, young and often stuck in body, twirling, clapping, smiling. The nursing-home staff would stand around and, after shaking their heads, join in. The residents would call out, "My turn. My turn." Then, after the mayhem, the program would end with ceremonial handshakes while I played the piano.

Touch by touch, in a moment or two of freedom, young and old and crippled could still dance with grace.

lexandria, in her mid-twenties, had leukemia. She had come from Greece with her mother, and neither of them could speak English. Apart from the few Greek words and phrases the staff learned and a Greek dictionary, we could not communicate through language.

When I first met Alexandria, I found her and her mom listening to a song on a cassette tape. I noticed that certain words in the song were repeated. I pronounced one of them, shrugged my shoulder and eyebrows, as if to ask, "What does this mean?" Alexandria's mom, understanding my mime, began to flap her arms. The song was about a bird. We were communicating! For the next few minutes, the three of us talked in mime.

An idea struck me. Music, they say, is the universal language. I would write a simple song for Alexandria:

Alexandria, smile.

Alexandria, we love you.

Alexandria, we're your friends.

Through our mime game, I would translate the lyrics into Greek. First, for the word smile, I placed fingers on either side of my mouth and grinned. Then I shrugged, again to ask, "What is this in Greek?" Alexandria and her mom conferred and agreed on a word, which I phonetically recorded on paper. For the next word, love, I hugged myself. They talked and agreed on another word. For the next word, friends, I hooked my forefingers together. Immediately, Alexandria's mom produced a word.

I now had all the words I needed. Using a rhythm and style similar to that of the song I had heard on the cassette, I sang the lyrics. Alexandria and her mother smiled politely, exchanging glances I could not quite interpret. A little later a woman who spoke both Greek and English entered Alexandria's room. Again I sang the words, this time feeling a little proud. When the woman began to laugh, I felt a bit indignant. Then, she explained to me what I had really sung:

Alexandria, show your teeth.

Alexandria, you're cold,

Alexandria, you're all tangled up.

Even Alexandria laughed, probably for the first time in a long time. Through human barriers and pride, such grace.

Chapter Six

The Cacophony of Cancer

Fermata (hold)

Things were growing in me: fulfillment, guilt, another baby, restlessness, cancer. All at once, all of it wrapped around me, like the moss that suffocates trees in the deep South, and I felt the chill of a new reality: life is short, shorter than we might know. And when I could get beyond that realization, the question loomed, What is important?

It was a strange time, this eclectic mix of emotion and substance: love and protoplasm, purpose and wild cells, devotion and creeping death. I didn't know about the cancer, not then, four months pregnant with our second child. But I intuitively sensed something was not right, something that felt like running in a lightning storm. I couldn't put my finger on it, really, but it was there underneath all my successes, what I thought I needed in life.

What I knew for sure certainly provided no proof. That's what I tried to tell myself. I dismissed the lump; I had had four previous surgeries to remove benign cysts from my breasts. My chest looked like a road map, one that had led me, falsely, into many alarming states of mind. I had fibrocystic disease; lumps came often. I had had one in my throat and on my lip; both had been benign. I began to resign myself to the fact, to relax.

That wasn't what was troubling me. I was also growing:

105

developing and using my God-given talents, gaining confidence, changing mostly for the better. At my job at the developmental center, I saw an endless string of miracles, some that even made my husband cry, some that, miracle of miracles, made me begin to believe in myself. To think that I could actually make a significant impact through the giving of myself. That I, IQ 106, had *something* to give.

So why in the middle of this joy was there this guilt, this restlessness, this thing that was eating at me? Part of it was Curtis, our second child, growing in my womb. Ernest, my husband, had never been terribly excited that I worked outside the home. But I had never neglected Martin for my job; I worked when he was in school. What would happen with the birth of our second child, a totally dependent baby? How could I justify working to my family's neglect? Yet how could I go back after having experienced so much, after feeling so channeled into God's grace?

Part of it was that I was jealous of Ernest. I felt that it was an unspoken assumption that he, who had it all—work *and* family, love *and* respect—did not want to share the work load at home. If I felt the need to work, to do my thing, then I would have to do it on top of my responsibilities at home. That was it. I wanted him to sacrifice a little for me. After all, I felt I had given up a great deal for him. I wanted him at least to understand how it felt for me to be snatched up from one environment—my college world where I was creative, respected, and connected—to this completely new environment, which offered me no challenge outside the home. Ernest, on the other hand, demanded that I be content. Back then, we were both so selfish.

Yet at the same time I blamed him less, respected him more. I realized that my perspective of his work—one filled with purpose, self-respect, admiration of peers—was awkwardly naïve. My own work taught me that even the rose garden has thorns: exhaustion, frustration, broken dreams, and, especially for a black man, unspeakable barriers. Ernest's world of work, once perfect in my mind, was coming into a more real focus: good *and* bad, of course.

Part of the restlessness was the tension that always comes with growth. I was a changing person. I started to have confidence, to show myself a little respect. I was feeling a little more me. I do not consider myself a wielder of power and position, and what I was doing was not purposely threatening. But even when Ernest cried at one of my stories, he knew that I had changed and that he, on whom I had relied as a primary source of fulfillment, would also have to change. Our lives demanded a new balance. I am thankful that he also was growing as he tried to start his own business and that we, in our separate strengths, grew together. It's just that I presented myself, my new self, in some rather subtle and uncompromising ways.

I waited too long to take action, to deal with these things that were growing in me. I just moved along, working hard, going through labor, nursing Curtis, returning to part-time work, nurturing a family, a grudge, and a spreading cancer. I didn't have the lump on my breast removed until a year after Curtis was born—nearly eighteen months after I had first noticed it. At first, I rationalized: I didn't want to go under an anesthetic while I was carrying Curtis. Then after his birth I gambled, and forgot: It was just a lump, not that serious. My life was full of lumps; that's just the way it had to be. Nothing to worry about.

I finally had the surgery, and one week later I went in to have the stitches removed after school. It was a thing on my to-do list, like picking up a coat from the dry cleaners. The doctor, after finishing and giving me an odd little glance, asked me to dress and come into his office. I noticed a chill run through me, the cut of his words. He sat there, his frame lanky in a leather-back chair, with shortly cropped gray hair and a white jacket. When I entered, he held his head down and rustled through some papers on his large wooden desk, as if distracted. A ruse, I thought. I sat in one of two chairs at the front of his desk, wanting it to swivel, even though I felt frozen, stuck in something. I noticed the overwhelming browns and grays: the carpet, the bookshelves, the certificates, the figurines, which were all the more colorless in the artificial light. His smile, a short one of recognition, was flat.

He handed me a paper. As I looked at it, I heard him mumble something, which I can't recall today, maybe: "Here are the test results. I'm sorry." The paper said: *breast carcinoma*. That's all, just two little words. Nothing else: no explanation, no preparation, no comforting remarks. Just the brown-grayness of his dark office and those fifteen small letters. I knew the doctor was watching me, expecting a reaction. And I tried. The performer in me sensed a stage, an opportunity to show the strength of my character, to show my colors. But there was nothing, a kind of nothing in the lungs, as if the wind had been knocked out of me.

Nothing, for the longest time. Finally, surprising even me, I heard a voice, small and petrified, say, "Where do we go from here?"

That was all the doctor needed. He slipped into gear. "Here is a list of people who could give you a second opinion." Breast carcinoma. *Cancer*. The real thing. "Here is a picture of the man I would recommend." I felt minuscule, cold, watched from the corner of an eye. "I'll photocopy this page, if you would like." *Cancer*. I noticed that my hands were shaking; I wondered if my legs would be able to carry me out of his office. "You'll need to set up an appointment soon." Two little words, a scrap of paper, almost weightless.

I composed myself, arranging this dull chaos, forcing myself to settle down, down, down, forcing whatever remained of me into my feet, so I could take a step, so unsure of my balance, my gravity, in this new world. Would I fall or rise? Was this an ending or a warped beginning? What could this possibly mean: this kind of two-word announcement that could suck me out of myself, out of time, out of the blue, and leave me there, in the middle of nowhere, to watch myself beside myself?

I felt myself move on into the receptionist's office. I knew she knew, could feel it in the way her eyes traced the shaky numbers appearing on my check as I virtually willed them into existence. *So this is pity,* I may have sensed, hoping that trembling hands could work an everyday magic. I walked outside, wanting things to be business as usual, my head frying in a blaze of kaleidoscopic color, seeing nothing, feeling little, my eyes swollen with the brown of the doctor's office, the gray in his hair and voice.

I remember nothing of the drive home. To my husband and my two children.

I got busy at letting go of the *why* question. I really worked at it and called it grace. I was determined not to let this thing fall in on me; I felt I had the strength for anything but that. I would risk all but my sanity or at least feeling that out of control. Instead of questioning, I looked for little answers, like the look in my husband's eyes when I told him of the cancer. It was late in the evening, following an open house at my school, and Ernest was getting ready to go to bed. I sat on the couch and patted the other end. I told him matter-of-factly, as if I needed a sore tooth pulled, completely without melodrama. I sat quietly, waiting for his response.

I don't know if I betrayed myself, if Ernest could sense my panic. It wasn't so much the cancer that scared me but how Ernest would react to that fact. I looked at him closely, beyond his eyes, the once-or-twice-in-a-lifetime hunger to know, really know, that he loved me that deeply. I looked for even a trace of rejection or repulsion. I could live with cancer, but not with a man who might not want me or who might find it difficult to be as much a part of me as he had been before. I didn't want to be tolerated; I needed to be loved, here and now.

I don't remember what Ernest said, but his look said, "I'll do this. Out of love." I told him to expect one of two things: either the lump or the breast would be removed. His eyes said, "Okay."

He asked me what my greatest fear was. I replied, without

thinking, "Watching the hurt in your eyes." Still trying to please, absently focused on the needs of others.

Ernest is, by profession and wiring, an architect: gifted and trained in economy, efficiency, mathematical thinking. He uses science and not often emotions as the tools for constructing a solution. His tears, therefore, took a while. It was in the routine of the following morning—the kids fed, clothes laid out—that he caught my glance, and his voice started to shake, only slightly. I hugged him; he hugged me. He cried. It was a clean kind of weeping that washed both of us.

I waited until the surgery date was set to tell my parents. I cringed at the thought of calling them; they had already lost brothers and sisters on both sides of my family to cancer. I didn't want to hurt them. I asked them both to get on the phone; I was technical, cool, almost professional, and I didn't use the word *cancer*. No talk of knives or emotions. I was so careful, in fact, that I was misleading. My sister, Deborah, told me later that after the call, Mother and she had started to cry. Confused, my daddy said, "What's the matter with you all?" My mother had to make clear what I had left vague: *cancer*. I regret that now, the pain that those tearless moments must have added to my father's grief.

The next day I got an early-morning phone call. It was my daddy. He said that he had just put my mom on a bus; she had insisted. That was, I knew, not in keeping with my mother's character; she didn't like to be intrusive. I was angry, at least as angry as I had ever been. I was back at work, busy at keeping down my emotions, afraid of what might happen, of what kind of drowning I might do if I allowed myself to slip into what had flooded me. Mom carried with her the threat of feeling. Even though I had never been confrontive with my mom, I had planned on the way to the bus station the best way to be upset with her. I think I had worked up a speech. When I got there, my fire prepared, I couldn't say anything but "Thanks." The way she looked, stood, moved—every ounce of her spoke of her love for me, her hurt. With one look I realized that she had to be there, tenderly stepping off that Greyhound, because she had no choice.

As we awaited my surgery, which was about a week away, we talked about my cancer. She never cried; she only wanted to help. At one point during the week, she said to me, "Daughter, you ask that doctor if he could take some of mine." Meaning part of her, part of one of her breasts. I realized then the size of the heart she possessed and now was willing to give away.

A few days before surgery, I decided to tell our older son, Martin, who was ten. I didn't really know what to say to him, but I didn't want him to find out from someone else. I was controlled but direct. "Martin, I have to go to the hospital. Part of me is very sick, and the doctors are going to take the sick part out. I'll be home in a few days. I want you to know that it's called cancer in case you hear other people talking about it. Are you okay with that? Do you have any questions?"

Martin, with the genes of an architect, asked in a kind of scientific curiosity, "Mommy, are you going to feel like half a woman?"

It did not take me back. "No," I answered directly. "I am more than my body parts."

It was hardest in some ways with Curtis, who was only a year old. The day before the surgery, it really hit me, as I was looking in the mirror. One breast would be gone. How would I explain it to my baby, this absence, when he went to suck? My symmetry, the life-giving balance that I had carefully nurtured, would never be the same.

I was in control.

Grace, for me, had always meant maintaining dignity under pressure. I admired the coolness of someone who pulled another person from a fire—the precision of a dancer, the steadiness of feet, a regulated engineer. More often than not, I have had to force that kind of grace, which in the forcing often ceases to be graceful. I am by nature too much a performer, playing with the fire of my own emotions, too given to drama. But unlike a performance, this was real. The theory of death ceased to be a theory, took on flesh and skull and bone, and stared at me from my bedroom ceiling late at night, a grisly incarnation.

I knew that if I let it, the thought would overwhelm me. *Cancer. Something eating me alive, inside out.* It was not so much the physical threat, which was real, but the potential for emotional trauma, the thought-by-thought, nerve-by-nerve, thread-by-thread unraveling of reality. Serious madness.

I was afraid of God, not that he was disciplining me out of anger, but that he wanted to shake me with a terrible and true love. The kind of love Jesus hinted at when he talked about suffering, those unpretty, unframed verses that we never hang above the kitchen stove. God became for me unpredictable. I didn't know what he might do, what dead-as-night road he might lead me down. I couldn't bear the thought of feeling that lost. So I chose to stay in control. I chose it in each common moment, as you might choose a red sweater over a blue one or ballroom dancing over trampolining.

I did all the right things, or at least the things that seemed right. I didn't question God. This was his will—was there any doubt about that? How could I buck against the fatness of that fact? What right did I have? It was up to me simply to ask for grace and then make it happen, to appropriate it in the correct measure, over the long haul.

I needed to fill the vacuum. I wanted facts, as many as I could get, about breast cancer: only one in ten dies, derived from epithelial tissue, cholesterol and cancer, exercise and cancer, insecticides and cancer, chromosomes and cancer. I wasn't obsessed with it, merely pushing back the darkness, occupying my mind the best I could.

I went back to work, finding grace and beauty in the smallest of movements. I worked and focused, worked and focused until I could think of little else. I could get lost at work in a good way, I thought, until cancer would be just a pinprick on the horizon, like a first star, hardly anything at all.

At home I lived in a curious afterglow of diagnosis. It was, at the same time, a thanksgiving and a bargaining. It was not hard for me to look at each new day as a gift to be treasured or as a chip to be played. In either case, what was demanded of me was that I be good. That I not scream at the children, that I hug them with sincerity and consistency, that I open up to my husband. The cancer, if nothing else, should teach me to live right, to be right, so that maybe in the grace of it, nothing else would go wrong. For the life of me, I couldn't tell the difference between courage and begging.

At night, fearing the silence and needing therapy, I washed myself in music: meandering, ethereal, without defined rhythm, over and over, through my worst nightmare, the break of notes on a distant shore.

All the way through, I stayed in control. As they wheeled me into surgery, I remember smiling and waving at everyone, Dad, Mom, Ernest, and the anesthesiologist, trying to put everyone at ease. I had accepted what the doctors had to say about what to expect: the scar, the loss of muscle and skin, the possible loss of range of motion in my left arm. I knew what to expect, and I relaxed in the certainty of the surgery: the strong definitions of the who, what, where, when, and why.

As I awoke after the surgery, even in the fog of the anesthesia, I remember hearing my mother's words, "It's over. Are you awake? Do you hear me?" I remember having the presence of mind to throw my arm over my head to test my mobility, to take immediate relief in that fact that so far, no damage. My mother mistook my exercise of control for delirium. *Still drugged,* I saw her think. I noticed I had perspired a good deal, and I worried about that, fussed with myself. The ultimate bad hair day.

The next few days saw a steady stream of doctors, standing in their white coats at antiseptic distances. I had had my surgery at a teaching hospital; I was not surprised that they came in groups of five or six, like a pack of trick-or-treaters. What I was surprised by was the way they talked and moved, like spectators at a golf course, all hushed and secretive and nerdy, muttering in statistics and their graphite lingo.

They were there to learn about me, to study me, to observe me. I knew that this was their job. It was simply asking for the moon to think that they should care. But when they didn't, it bothered me. How can you teach people medicine without teaching them to care? Each of the residents tried to get my doctor to move quickly during the rounds, even when he had my test results, so that they could move on to the next case: the prostate in 109 or the Parkinson's in 103.

I had to ask my doctor for my results. "Oh, yeah, yeah. Let's see. One of the lymph nodes was involved of the nine we took out." The words "one was involved" stuck in my head, like the lyrics of a bad song, like a sociology professor describing a dating relationship: *one was involved.*

The cancer, in other words, had spread.

I had feared that, but I feared even more the type of treatment I would need. I hated the thought of chemotherapy—losing my hair, my weight, my food, my composure, a real and indescribable part of me. It was determined that with only one lymph node of nine involved, it wasn't necessary for chemotherapy or radiation. I was to have a checkup once every three months.

"And one other thing," the doctor informed me, almost as an aside, "the cancer was estrogen-receptor positive." That meant that any estrogen that was in my body would nourish any cancer cells that remained. Within six weeks, they wanted me to have a oophorectomy. I had already lost one ovary during a miscarriage; now surgery would take the other one. It wasn't that we had any plans to have more children, but I didn't like the idea of having the choice taken from me, ripped from me, that is, as if it were an enemy. This was more than the taking of just a body part.

The oophorectomy was far worse than the mastectomy. What did it mean to lose all trace of what it meant to be a

114

woman? What did it mean in terms of hormones and hair and drying up? Would I trace a mustache? Would I have hot flashes? Would I ever feel comfortable, like slipping into silk, with what remained of my femininity? I didn't know. And the uncertainty, faceless as the unknown, stared me into a corner.

The recovery itself was difficult. The surgery was a few days before Christmas, and when I told my nurse that I wanted to be home for the holidays, she laughed at me, a Sarah laugh, brittle with years and unbelief, as if I might have had a better chance of giving birth. "What makes you think you are going to go home for Christmas?" That sneer brought me to myself, heralded a challenge. I was determined not to let this woman be right. Before the surgery, the doctor explained that he wanted to put a tube down my nose so that I would be sure to keep my food down. I politely said no. It would slow down my recovery. He agreed, but asked me to tell my nurse if I threw up. The next day after I vomited, I hid that little gray-brown, kidney-shaped bowl under my sheets. My nurse came scowling into my room: "What makes you think you are going to go home for Christmas?" I smiled at her as if she were St. Nicholas himself, and she never suspected a thing. This was a joyous conquering, a mean business. I still don't remember how I got rid of that bowl of spit-up food, what with me confined to my bed, but I do know that I was home, due to that nurse's spewed-out words, by Christmas.

That was the easy part. With the breast surgery, I was back at work within ten days. The oophorectomy, which felt more like a gutting, left me doubled over, a regular hunchback, confined to the couch and the springing of my thoughts. It was unwanted down time, buried in uselessness. What I thought might take two weeks took more like two months.

It was the kind of control that a person might feel fighting against a strong tide and with every ounce of energy, calling it a blessing that at least the scenery didn't change. I stayed in the

115

same spot, exhausted, but grateful that I still had an oar to dip in the water. Through control, through busyness, I kept my head from spinning into depths that I thought would overwhelm me and, all the time, letting the changes growing in me get swept away, rotting without my attention, washed up like winter carp on a beach at Easter. Later I learned that it was a mess I could not tiptoe through.

I wanted, begged, demanded that things return to normal. So I did the normal things. I worked, taught Sunday school, directed the church choir, did the laundry, made meals, took the kids places. I had gotten through the cancer, I thought, still mostly intact. I hadn't fallen into it.

I realize now that it was a lukewarm peace. When it comes to the concept of normal, God spits it out as he did Jonah, on a beach with seaweed between his toes, not yet broken, gifted but still reeking of whatever else floats in a whale's belly. That's where the agenda of self always lands, in such an exhausted and stinking mess.

It's not that the things I was doing were wrong. They were important, urgent, mostly honest, religious things. I was trying my best to cope. Most people, in fact, were amazed. "Deforia, how do you do it?" But good things, disconnected from an unconditional surrender to God's will, look more in the end like the faces of trouble, secret terror, and self-righteousness. But I didn't know that then.

But even then, in the directed motions of self, there were bolts of grace, unworked for, electrical, unflappable.

After my breast surgery, for example, I was placed in a hospital room with three other women, all of whom had recovered from breast cancer decades ago. They were in my room for unrelated problems, all proof that cancer does not have to be fatal, that this was not the end of things, that God's grace must still remain the focal point. It was the Lord's way of saying: "Look, look, and look."

Then, in the high art of an architect, there was Ernest. With me standing in front of the mirror, looking at the scar where my breast had been, I called him over: "Here, honey. Look at this."

116

He walked over, looked in the mirror, and said, "Okay." Without flinching. In his nondrama, a dramatic gesture of love and acceptance.

And Martin after school, "Can I get you something, Mom? Are you okay, Mom? Is there anything I can do for you, Mom?" He would bring me water and tea, and read me books. He was sweet, without being doting, professional like a nurse, but always caring. He knew that I needed help, and I knew that he was always there for me.

Grace came in the form of a woman from the church. Me, with one breast gone and my last ovary scheduled to go, she brought me a slinky negligee, the low kind with spaghetti straps. That gift, on the very day that they would take another feminine part, left me feeling supple, tender, caressable, distinctly female. Who would have the courage, the wisdom, to give such a gift?

I saw it in the way my pastor was shaken when I told him about the breast cancer. He, being a measured man, couldn't hide the hurt, didn't even try. His face grimaced, a quick, deep groan coming from his throat, and I knew he cared. As he recovered, he looked up at me and said, "Deforia, the Lord has something special for you out of this. You'll know down the line." What the minister said, the way the rock cracked for a second, left me with a solid promise.

Ten months later, after I thought things were back to normal, the cancer licked, I found another lump in the chest wall where the breast had been. That quickly, that big. I knew that I was in trouble. Deadly things were still growing in me.

What kind of grace was that?

*J*ohn was a fiercely angry six-year-old boy with leukemia. He hated the hospital, fought against the needles and nurses, and understood well the toughness of life.

The only things I knew about John before I visited him in his hospital room were that he had a brother named Rory and that he often threw things at people who came to visit him. When I arrived, I was greeted with a shower of liquid. At the same time, I heard something hit the floor beside me—John's bedpan.

I tried to appear undaunted, as if the stains on my blouse might be tears or punch or rain from the parking lot. "John, tell me three things about your brother, Rory, and I will get out of here fast," I began. John proceeded to relay three of the most disgusting facts that he could think of.

Still trying my best to appear unshaken, I asked him if he knew the song "Pop Goes the Weasel." When he seemed hesitant, I handed him a musical instrument that made loud noises when you slapped it hard. John was the type of child that loved to make loud noises. "I want you to slap this as hard as you can at the part that goes pop," I said. I improvised a song:

> Passes gas and picks his nose,
> And then he tries to hug me.
> He gets the mail, he bit my dog's tail.
> That's [pop] my brother, Rory.

As it turned out, John was so taken by the song that he asked if we could call his brother and sing the song over the phone to him and then record it on tape for his parents. I gladly agreed. It was the beginning of a great relationship.

Chapter Seven

Finding Healing in Faith, Community, and Music

Sostenuto *(sustained, prolonged)*

I lost control.

More than once—in the doctor's office, after a card from a friend, in the emptiness and uncertainty, in the unblinking stare of cancer. Me, the one who always prided herself in dignity, no matter how undignified the circumstances.

When the doctor examined the bean-sized lump, he said matter-of-factly, "I'll feel better when that's out of your chest and in a jar." That's all. I stopped him before he left. Here I was thinking I was getting better. I had this hope. And then I cried. My doctor, a gentle man, did not know what to say and left me in the room, staring into a mirror, watching the tears spill out of my eyes.

That was the beginning of what I had thought was the end. I was not well; the cancer had returned, maybe never really left. It didn't take a high IQ to read the writing on the wall; I had met so many people who, once the cancer returns, descend into surgery after surgery, the scalpel cutting, cutting, cutting, piece by piece by piece, less and less and less, until there is nothing left to cut, except a fleshy skeleton and then a corpse.

My optimism, which I drew from a deep well, had run dry.

So had my energy, my courage, my hope, my fortitude, my rage, my discipline, my always pleasing smile. I was at an end of myself.

Maybe for the first time in my life I had met a challenge I could not overcome. Hadn't I risen above my IQ to be accepted at one of the most prestigious music schools in the country? Hadn't I overcome the early disappointments and adjustments in my marriage? Hadn't I returned to school, studied until two o'clock in the morning, sent my child off to school every day, and beyond my wildest dreams landed a job as a music therapist? I knew that it was not I who had done this, not really, but I was fond of the mostly unspoken conjunction *and*. God *and* I. We had done this, these minor and major miracles, together, God *and* I.

I came to terms with this reality several weeks after surgery. I had just read a friend's greeting card, one on the order of Helen Steiner Rice, something spiritual and pretty. On that Tuesday afternoon, I sat alone in a chair, too tired to stay busy, and thought about death. I pictured the way the beautiful ones died on television, so peace-filled and wise, passing along with their final breath something elegant and everlasting instead of having their eyes and mouths open wide, gasping like a goldfish for one last breath of air. I thought about how I always felt that I was going to die young, even told my mother, who looked at me dumbfounded. I thought about destiny.

God *and* I. That was it. Fresh out of miracles it seemed. God *and* I. In the face of death, it's either that or nothing at all. There was no one to blame, no sign, no job, no certainty, no cure in sight, and no telling what God had in mind. I was alone with God, holy in his determined, unpredictable will. That was it, a place of both alarming aloneness and tender communion.

It was Ernest, in his love, without his really knowing it, who brought me to this abandoned place. He was the one who suggested that I slow down, take some time off, and not try to outrun it. He could tell that I was exhausted. He knew that my body needed a rest before it could heal.

And it was in the rest, in the terrifying ways that the hours froze one on top of the other, that I realized the extent of my restlessness. I stared at new realities, the things growing in me, malignant with tension. Feelings that I had always precisely juggled came crashing down on me. Questions that I had never asked—never even dared myself to think—fired out of my mouth in machine-gun staccato. At myself. At God. For two weeks, in the throw of questions, everything stopped and reality was redefined: colors changed, priorities shifted, cars hummed by. And I was lost, as lost as a child's voice pitched in a pitch black cave.

What did all of this mean? How was I going to deal with this? Could faith look into the eyes of death and not blink first? What did God want from me? What did the future hold? What would happen to Ernest and the boys if I died? Couldn't I have a sign, some reassurance that things would be okay, maybe not a note on the refrigerator, but at least less of the chill? What could I possibly do? Why was this happening?

I heard no answers, nothing concrete at least, nothing on which to build the foundation of a future. I felt betrayed, blank, abandoned, stripped.

Out of control.

This is what I had always feared: alone, with nothing to do; uncertain, with nothing to prove; challenged, beyond my capacity; sane, but for how long or even for what? I had always counted on parameters that showed me where the four walls were, what the proper manners are within those walls, who did what and when and why and how. Even in my relationship with God, I imagined a contract, a give-and-take, work-reward, parrot-cracker thing.

I needed the silver lines etched in a blueprint for living, the feeling of control in the precise twist of a compass or a plastic protractor, the certain and quantifiable angle of the lines. I needed a measured faith: direct the church choir; be there for Sunday school; tithe ten percent; be kind; don't doubt God. It was my way of staying regulated, of breaking down life into past and present and future. It was the clock to which I religiously set my life.

That kind of control, the teeth that gripped time, was the known confines of my relationship with God. *I could,* I would memorize, *do anything through Christ who strengthens me. But please, Lord, not this. Anything, that is, except this kind of anything, this kind of release—that in the end,* anything *may happen.*

I came back to the same words: lost, abandoned, naked, floating. Of course, I had Curtis, our baby, to snare me with his needs, to bring me back to the world of bottles and dishes and laundry, the cry and messy smile of humanity, the welcome and pardoning relief of routine. I had Martin, our eleven-year-old, who drew me in with his stories of math class and kickball. And I had Ernest, always there for me, just slightly out of reach, about the distance of my own arms.

But mostly, for once in my life, it was just God and me. I wish I could point to a moment or two, like Gethsemane or the Last Supper, and say, "This is when this happened, and this is where I learned that." It wasn't like that. Instead of points on a graph, it was a process, a line that traced itself into a figure eight, the symbol for eternity, the endless search for answers and direction.

I found myself giving up—or being stripped of—precious things, or things that I thought were precious. For the most part I gave up the need to feel as if I had to please and be pleased by everyone. I didn't perform well; I had no reason to. How could I be on a stage when somewhere on a hospital shelf a jar labeled me: *Lane, Deforia: breast carcinoma*? Maybe the jar stood right next to the jar with my first tumor, maybe with a spot reserved for the next one, and the next one. *Encore, encore* were not exactly the words that I cared to hear. I simply had no need for them. The buzzing of my own thoughts made me either unaware or unconcerned about what others thought or said I was. That was, for a person always focused on approval, a grace of this disease.

I found myself giving up—or at least being willing to give up—my work. For so long I had struggled with the tension between my part-time work and my questions about whether I should stay at home full time with our children. Caught in the uncertainty between purpose and selfishness, talent and family, respect and need, love and duty, I was tired of wrestling with the tangled-up feelings of guilt and dignity. Right in the middle of this, I heard a *Focus on the Family* broadcast in which James Dobson said that if mothers didn't stay home with their children, the children would be lost by the age of five. Now that I knew what lost felt like, I didn't want to pass it along to our child. I wrestled: *God, I'm willing to quit, but why do you keep sending me miracles at work, genuine touches of your grace? Show me your will, clearly, and I'll do it.*

I found myself giving up my own body. With what the cancer ate and the knife cut away, I felt incomplete, confused. I had a difficult time not feeling that in some way my body, this temple of the Holy Spirit, had become the enemy. What could cause such a personal mutiny, what deep and secret thing?

And then—and I want to say this as undramatically as possible—I found myself willing to give up my life to cancer, to God. It wasn't that I no longer cared. It was the same kind of I-don't-give-a-rip attitude that I carried into certain auditions—those few times when I was unconcerned about the outcome, when my voice unclenched and found the high notes, when the music would stun me and others with its purity, transcendence. It was the kind of abandon I felt when I had not defiled the music with myself—my need to use it for my own ends—but had accepted it as a gift and through what was uniquely me had given it back, with reverence and joy. This time it was not my voice that I was being asked to release, but my life. It was a gift from God, too, wasn't it?

I don't want this to sound too pious or sentimentally spiritual; whatever this process entailed, it was certainly not devout or sweet. I was really frightened. These days were filled with the peculiar and strangling frenzy of waiting. I cried a lot, worried a lot, questioned a lot, felt lost a lot, slept little, and beyond all of that, God began to touch me deeply.

I started being honest, dreadfully honest. I felt the freedom to do not just the right thing, but the *real* thing. I didn't like the idea of death. Death is, for me, the great intruder, the beast that none of us cares to acknowledge, much less name, even though it shamelessly prowls, big as an elephant, in front of all our eyes. I was angry with God that he would ask me even to consider it, this weird beast.

I had questions, mean questions for which I didn't think God had the answers, or if he did, he wasn't willing to share them with me. And when I asked those questions, a surprising thing happened: what was meant as confrontation became release. Far from resenting my questions, God welcomed them. He bore the pain in the questions just as Christ bore the cross. In my confusion, I may have wanted to wound him, but he only bled for me. In expressing what was really going on inside me— the anger, hurt, the rage against dying—he comprehended my pain and translated my helplessness into a certain strength. I don't know how. I don't know much about such grace.

In my cry of despair was the wild stirring of hope. Moses' prayer in Psalm 90 became my prayer:

Lord, you have been our dwelling place
 throughout all generations.
Before the mountains were born
 or you brought forth the earth and the world,
from everlasting to everlasting you are God.
You turn men back to dust,
 saying, "Return to dust, O sons of men."
For a thousand years in your sight
 are like a day that has just gone by,
 or like a watch in the night.
You sweep men away in the sleep of death;
 they are like the new grass of the morning—
though in the morning it springs up new,
 by evening it is dry and withered.
We are consumed by your anger
 and terrified by your indignation.
You have set our iniquities before you,
 our secret sins in the light of your presence.
All our days pass away under your wrath;

124

> we finish our years with a moan.
> The length of our days is seventy years—
> or eighty, if we have the strength;
> yet their span is but trouble and sorrow,
> for they quickly pass, and we fly away.

> Who knows the power of your anger?
> For your wrath is as great as the fear that is due you.
> Teach us to number our days aright,
> that we may gain a heart of wisdom.
> Relent, O LORD! How long will it be?
> Have compassion on your servants.
> Satisfy us in the morning with your unfailing love,
> that we may sing for joy and be glad all our days.
> Make us glad for as many days as you have afflicted us,
> for as many years as we have seen trouble.
> May your deeds be shown to your servants,
> your splendor to their children.

> May the favor of the Lord our God rest upon us;
> establish the works of our hands for us—
> yes, establish the work of our hands.

God and I. And in the dropping of the I, just God. That was it, no answers, no specifics on a night beach, no concluding refrain. Just the letting go of it, all of it, and in the release, in the dying itself, the seed of hope. I know it sounds backward, but I have found that the deepest moments in my life have always been the least contrived. In the release of control, I have found humbling power. In the chaos, I have found moments of sustaining peace.

God gave no answers, then, just his presence. Just that. And his grace was sufficient.

Paradox is befuddled language. Jesus constantly perplexed us with paradox: "I tell you the truth, unless a kernel of wheat falls to the ground and dies, it remains only a single seed. But if it dies, it produces many seeds. The man who loves his life will lose it, while the man who hates his life in this world will keep it for eternal life" (John 12:24–25).

I don't even pretend to know all of what these words mean, the depth of reality that they dive, but I have learned this: death is not something we do just once. Not if we are living right. For it was in my little deaths along the way—my *needs* for control, certainty, position, respect, and even life itself—that I found what I was looking for. It was a dying not necessarily to the things I did but to *why* I did them. Sin is always this: whatever clings, suffocates. I am not saying that this is easy, not without the enormous energy of faith, drenched in a night sweat of fear, like Moses at the edge of the sea, bloodthirst on every side, when suddenly and powerfully the water parts.

Where there was once mud, solid ground. From slavery, a path of escape. The answer *is* the presence of God.

I wandered, like Israel in the wilderness, between faith and hunger, emancipation and fear, the odd need to go back and the hesitancy to move forward. I wanted the moments of fellowship to last, to wipe away my tears, to dry up my fear, to rake in my anger, to untighten the knot in my stomach. But the huge moments of grace came and went, leaving me to my puny self. I lost myself in the psalms, the spirituals, the ancient rhythms, the blood and decibels and pulse of the words. In them I found the ring of truth, the music of grace.

I remember one tear-filled day spent pacing side to side, back and forth, like a Bengal in a zoo. I finally sat down at the piano to calm myself. I didn't know what to do with myself, so I played. I opened the hymnbook to a song I had not heard before and unleashed myself:

> I've been through the fire;
> I've been through the flood.
> I've been through the valley,
> I've been through the fire.
> I've walked through deep water,

I've bowed in the mire,
I've fought in the battle
With courage all gone;
But this is the reason
I always go on.
Jesus is with me,
My shepherd and guide.
All I have needed his hands will provide,
That makes a difference.
This friend by my side;
Jesus is walking with me.

The music flowed, words to eyes to mind to heart to soul to fingers, like the river in an artery, fluid and pulsing, laced with what was necessary. It was an odd movement, the way the music connected with me; even though I had never seen the notes before and was not particularly good at sight reading, I played the song as if I had known it intimately all of my life. This friend by my side, Jesus, is walking with me. In the music, in the way my faith danced, Jesus was there, marking more than my time.

It was in this ebb and flow, the tension between what was and what might be, that I died my little deaths. In a sense, I had no choice; that was the demanding and terrible grace of it. Die to fear or go insane. Die to a need for a future or start living in the agony of sentences passed. Die to power and position, for what strength is there in an underground plot? Die to selfish desires, for what could be more selfish, more desperate, than demanding to live? The choices were both quite simple and exceedingly difficult. It was only as I moved in faith, one tiny step, that I found the grace to move again, another tiny step. I had to die so that I could live.

I was, through all the kicking and screaming, finally willing. That was it. God arranged the rest.

There was grace in Ernest, always earnest. The way he asked

me, in the middle of my fear for my family, a difficult question: "Honey, do you know where you will go when you die?" It made me angry, the way it felt like an accusation.

I said the obvious. "I'd be absent from the body, at home with the Lord." Of course. Even a baby in the faith could say that.

Ernest spoke again. "Honey, if the Lord loves you that much—for you to be in heaven with him—if he died so that you could live eternally, what makes you think that he loves the boys and me any less?" A much better question, charged with a predetermined answer.

I finally learned to open up with Ernest, consider his deepest feelings. I had joined an American Cancer Society breast-cancer support group so that I could talk with people who understood, who shared the same feelings, thoughts, fears, and hopes. During one meeting, an amateur theater group presented a series of dramas dealing with the reality of cancer. In one of the sketches, a man much like my husband was talking to another person about his wife's illness and stumbled consistently on the word *cancer*. That got me thinking about how Ernest must be feeling about all of this. I rarely talked about the cancer with Ernest, knowing that he was private with his feelings. I told myself that I wanted to spare him the awkwardness; in reality, I was just being selfish. It was me, not Ernest, whom I wanted to spare.

So we talked, husband and wife, and that was the beginning of a new direction, a way out of the fear. It was time for me to stop thinking about me and turn my attention to Ernest's needs. His concerns were the mortgage, insurance, all the nuts-and-bolts things that he was drawn to think about. It was a breakthrough, not so much in easing his fears, but in the fact that cancer no longer completely shut me in, shut me down. In genuine concern for my husband, I had poked a hole through the fear and self-absorption, and in the connection the hole started a slow leak in the pressure of the disease.

But mostly it was God's grace: the kind that falls direct from heaven, the manna, the kind that you can actually sink

1. Most people seem surprised when I tell them I frowned a lot as a baby!

2. Following graduation from high school, I was chosen to be a voice major at University of Cincinnati College Conservatory of Music.

3. My parents worked hard to provide an environment of love and safety for me, Howard, and Deborah.

4. A precious family photo—the last before my father died.

Listening to my mother play her piano instilled an early love for music in my sister, Deborah, and me.

1. College was a swirl of endless practices and intense competitions.

2. Home for spring break, I harmonized with my sister and friends at a church program.

3. As a junior, I found that I loved to perform. Here I am with my goofy stage husband in the comic opera *Gianni Schicchi,* and as the lead in Puccini's *Suor Angelica* (background).

1. Ernest and I were married on January 4, 1972, at this little chapel on Stewart Air Force Base.

2. I was immediately drawn to Ernest's quiet strength and sense of purpose.

3. The men in my life have given me many years of joy. (l to r: Ernest, Martin, and Curtis.)

4. As a first-time mother, I was amazed by Martin and would sometimes sit and watch him sleep.

5. Our second son, Curtis—already enjoying music!

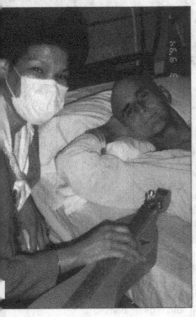

1. Many patients look forward to their music session as a welcome break from daily hospital routine.

2. The children get a lesson in rhythm sticks during a 5 West group music therapy session at Rainbow Babies and Childrens Hospital.

3. Our hospital team meets each morning to review cases and map out our day.

4. Parents enjoy watching me work with their children—and often join in!

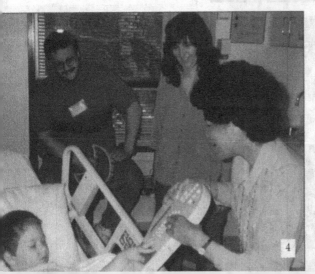

1. I took the Raub Development Center's sing-and-sign choir "on the road," caroling in malls, high schools, and nursing homes.

2. My "she"ro, Mrs. Harry C. (Thelma) Wentworth, has shared words of wisdom at many points in my life and career.

3. I often asked the talented staff at the Raub Center to help me perform mini-concerts for the kids.

4. Traveling throughout the country as a spokesperson for the American Cancer Society has been a richly rewarding experience.

Music holds the power to touch the
hearts of children with God's grace.

1. As part of our Musicians in Residence program, students from the Cleveland Institute of Music come to play for our patients room to room.

2. The University Hospital Singers came dressed as the "Rainbow Raisinettes" to entertain the children and parents.

your teeth into, the not-in-a-million-years, undeserved stuff. As the breast-cancer support group, called I Can Cope, wound down, I asked if I could write a song and sing it at the final meeting. Judy MacKintosh, the social worker who led the group, liked the idea.

Thirty minutes before that final meeting, I was sitting on the toilet, frantically trying to compose the song. *I can't keep putting things off until the last minute,* I told myself. I came up with something, a song entitled "We Can Cope," and was surprisingly pleased. I rushed off, never dreaming of the wake that this song would make in my life. I sang it that night among tears and hugs and exclamations. People were deeply touched.

Within a week, I got a call from the American Cancer Society. They had heard about the song from someone in the group, and they wanted to hear it. I made an appointment to sing it. They also loved it. They asked me to compose a few more verses and indicated that they might want me to record the song. I went home, finished a few verses—this time on a piano stool, not a toilet stool—and knew, as I rarely do, that this was right. Although they asked me not to sing about religion, to keep it "universal," I believed the second verse of the song was inspired by God.

Life has its up and downs we know,
Not always fair but still we go
From day to day seeking ways to make it better.
So we strive on and on, sometimes sighing or singing a
  song,
But if there's a lesson we have learned, it's "We can cope!"

Chorus
We can cope! We can cope!
If there's a lesson we have learned, it's "There is hope!"
We can cope! We can cope!
If there's a lesson we have learned, it's "We can cope!"

It's true that the things that cause us pain
Give birth to new strength we can't explain.

129

It dares us to fight, convinces the soul that life is worth
living.
It's then that we rise and risk we may fall,
Pressing on and heeding life's call.
Our living becomes an example to all—We can cope!
It's time to look up and laugh and live,
Time to say "yes," join hands, and give.
The future looks grand, for we understand together we'll
make it.
This race can be won, the victory's in view;
Impossible dreams are known to come true.
Look out world! We're winning and we're coming
through.
We can cope!

The American Cancer Society asked me to record the song,
which began, strangely enough, with thirty minutes, a toilet,
and a flush of grace. And they say that God doesn't have a
sense of humor. The next thing I knew I was in a posh record-
ing studio, surrounded by long-haired jazz musicians with
their digital instruments and eyes on the clock. I had brought
along a handful of music therapists and church musicians, violin, trumpet, and piano players and wondered what in the
world I was doing. We laid down the drum track with the two
long-hairs in forty-five minutes. They seemed eager to get
somewhere, what with this being a free gig and all. Then we,
the called-together ones, overlaid the rest of the tracks—piano,
violin, trumpet, then guitar. Finally, I sang on top of it all. It was
a thrilling experience taut with energy, community, and message. The song became a theme song of sorts for the American
Cancer Society; they played it across the country in support
groups and society meetings.

From there, the dominoes started to fall. I began to speak.
During a talk I gave at the Cleveland Clinic for their annual
Cancer Survivors' Day, the executive director of the American
Cancer Society, Russell Catanese, was in the audience. He
decided on the spot that he wanted me to begin speaking

nationally. He contacted the American Cancer Society's national office and put me on the Celebrities Against Cancer list. I'm sure he recommended me for a variety of reasons—I had had cancer, I was a performer, I could sing, I was black—all of those surely figured into the formula, but mostly it was manna from heaven, inexplicable and supernatural grace.

Soon Ernest and I found ourselves lodged in plush hotels—the kinds with mirrored walls, chandeliers that broke light into rainbows, and marble fountains—free of charge. This was all part of being named to the Celebrities Against Cancer speaking tour. We felt so guilty, or maybe just so conditioned to thrift, that we took along peanut butter sandwiches and apples so that we didn't spend money on fancy dinners. "On us," they had said, and finally after a few pinches we believed them. The American Cancer Society is a sophisticated set of people who know where and how to raise money for a critical cause. They know not only what plays in Peoria, but also what plays among the privileged few.

Should I say that I went with it or that I was swept away by it? One moment I had been unraveling in desperation, cling-ing to a #2 thread of faith, just the tiniest imaginable string between life and death, and then after thirty minutes on a toilet seat, I was in Boston, Los Angeles, Fort Lauderdale, cradled in respect, life, value, and almost embarrassing comfort. Who could imagine such a thing, such a reversal, in the desert, such a wild, blood-red blossoming of grace?

Not everything, however, was coming up roses. Although the cancer disappeared (it has remained in remission since 1982), I still had scars. I still had the emptiness of having given so much: a breast, an ovary, a chunk of scar, a piece here, a piece there, my hope, my control. I still felt the way the clown, Death, played with my insides—beyond the tissues and cells and inci-sions. I made the choice of God one between outrage or des-perate clinging, hating any hint of laughter, my faith slipping off like icicles in spring, one dangerous sliver at a time, until all that remained seemed like nothing, just a shred. What could fill that kind of emptiness, that vacuum of spirit? Who could replace the pieces that were missing? In more ways than one, I felt a continuing absence in body and spirit.

I couldn't talk about that at one of my speeches for the American Cancer Society. It had to happen at church a few years later, among believers, in the fluorescent shadow of a cross. They had come to hear my story, jammed to the last row in the balcony. I was shaken by the turnout: What could I possibly have to say to so many people? I still knew so little about how God moved, mysteriously, in and beyond each one of us. I related, in total, my experience with breast cancer, about what it took and what it left. I spoke of deep loss, the way I felt empty, dismantled, a piece here, a piece there.

Then I read some verses from 2 Corinthians. Even though parts were missing from my body, Christ did not see me as only leftover fragments. I was, and am, complete in him. It was only then, after the emptiness was filled, that I could fully acknowledge God. I sang a song I had written, "My Soul Is Complete in Christ." I dedicated it to Ernest, my faithful and solid husband. My voice cracked slightly when I caught Ernest's eye in the balcony. I watched the way his head slumped in love, and I began to sing.

There have been times my soul cried out for your mercy
  and your care.
It seems my life has seen its share of heartache and despair.
But then I think of your son Jesus Christ: how he suffered,
  bled, and died.
He's my daily bread, the lifter up of my head.
My soul is complete in Christ.
My soul is complete in Christ.
My soul is complete in Christ.
It's nothing I have done;
It's by the grace of God's Son.
My soul is complete in Christ.
I want to be a living sacrifice
Holy and acceptable to you.
I want to think on whatsoever things

Are pure and just and true.
I'll take the shield of faith and the sword of truth.
I know my battle has been won.
One day I'll see my King, and I'll rejoice as I sing,
My soul is complete in Christ!

That was when I began to understand, in the tears and break of the Holy Spirit that followed: God is in control, not you, not me, not really.

Eli, a Jewish man in his sixties, was dying. He was alone, having grown away from all his children. Each time I came to see him, he had grown worse and worse.

Eli was a successful man in many ways; financially, he had done very well. When I asked him, gently, if he would like to make peace with his children, he would talk about the shopping mall that he was going to build. The greater his decline, the more he would talk about his shopping mall, the less about his children. He seemed quite oblivious to the fact that the only groundbreaking that would occur in his name would be the earth turned for his cemetery plot.

Moments before he died, one of his sons entered with a preacher. I listened as they both screamed at Eli that he must be saved. I wondered if then, too, he wasn't thinking of his shopping mall.

Chapter Eight

Order and Grace: The Mathematics of Music

Legato (smoothly)

Symmetry, proportion, pattern, scales, harmony: even in a world gone wrong, there exists in or alongside or through the chaos a sense or ordering, a mathematical precision, a knowledge of certainty even into infinity, things you can count on, a reason, an unstoppable purpose behind the numbers.

The octave is the basic musical building block in much the same way the atom is the building block of whatever is tangible. Technically defined as the interval of eight diatonic degrees between two tones, one that has twice as many vibrations per second as the other, the octave is in a more profound sense nothing less than this: the harmony of the universe.

One ancient philosopher asked, "If the sounds of an octave could be expressed in harmonious proportions, why not also the harmony of the whole universe?" I'm not entirely sure what he meant by this. My own rather humble guess would be threefold: first, the things that are huge in life are small, fundamental; second, don't panic, there is in the order of things, an orderer; third, in some mysterious yet very precise ways, everything is connected, designed to be harmonious.

135

I'm not sure where cancer fits into all this, or for that matter, where viruses or noise or acid rain fit in, but it is indisputable that some laws are indisputable: a drop follows a rise, an action creates a reaction, water freezes at 32° F, and rivers return to the sea. No one outside an asylum would dispute the fact of facts: set, concrete, in balance, unchangeable.

In the year or two following the recurrence of my cancer, I became aware of a certain arrangement in life. First, with the cancer came the breathtaking reality that I did not possess the power even of my next breath. In my quest for control, I had fought against the reality of truth that I now understood without a doubt: *I was a dependent creature.* In a staredown with death, it is always certain who will blink first. In the totality of life, our power eventually and certainly unwinds, or as the psalmist says, "We wither like grass." This, I believe, is the still, small whisper of God, the Creator, the Sustainer. Second, I could see in the laws and immutable facts that govern our lives a hard-nosed and tender movement, the feel of a C note on a C note—call it unity or grace. Third, in the often wild, sometimes comical arrangement of law and grace, science and art, creator and creature, there is laughter, and who can define that?

I have already spoken of my loss of control. The cancer, if it must be considered some kind of warped gift, taught me a most valuable and profound lesson: my life was not my own. I call it a gift, when pressed to the wall, because I'm not sure I would have learned this lesson any other way. When I could give up seeing my life as under my own control, I found I suddenly had the ability to love without asking, to grasp the deep movement in a moment, to feel the electricity in a possibility, to give birth to an inexplicable strength. With the passing of time, of course, the lesson often fades, and I am left to believe that my well-being depends on my efforts. The lesson of dependence is one that I must learn over and over again.

The grace was everywhere: in the hues of "coincidence," in the palette of a sunset, in the love of my husband and children, in the way that I could look at myself in a mirror. How can I say this? Grace was, and is, the power to see things differently. Without even really trying, I began to look at myself and others more attuned to the art of giving than to the demand of science.

Through the suffering and fear in my bout with cancer, Ernest and I both learned of a fresh, almost exotic grace. It was in that most troubling time that I learned of the deep love Ernest had for me. I believe it was always there, but I had lacked the grace to understand or experience it. Sometimes it was no more than his taking me in his arms and holding me on the stairs or a look in his eyes; in either case, he held me with all his might, with all the power of his love. The power in those moments made me look to see if I had done, said, or worn something that prompted his giving. But as hard as I looked, I could find no particular motive.

It is just this: Ernest loves me, sometimes without reason. Such grace is infectious. When I began to see one thing differently, I began to see other things in a new light too. Ernest's love taught me of God's love. God loves us not because of what we do for him or how we look or the verse that we have memorized or how we sound in the choir or the shower. In my efforts to "press toward the mark" or "win the prize," I often confuse love for approval. In my desire to win the Father's love, I often feel compelled to do things to earn his favor. But God, like a righteous parent, loves his children just as they are, as well as for what they can become, and not for what his children can do for him. Our responsibilities, deeds, and works become not a method of manipulating love but a *response* to love.

Ernest and I, in the grace to see our love from a fresh perspective, began to make fewer demands on each other. Any two people in a relationship, especially two people as different in temperament and perspective as Ernest and I are, tend to want to make the other person more and more like one's own self. In the sameness comes comfort—but in the long run, also frustration and tedium. With the cancer, Ernest and I could no longer take each other for granted. As a result, we each came to see life as a gift of great value. We slowly came to understand that each of our lives was designed in a weave of great diversity, talent, and perspective. Our responsibility was not to attempt to clone our individual selves in our spouse but to create an environment in which each of us could fully realize the potential that God had built into our lives. For the most part, we stopped trying to force each other into a preconceived idea or the reflection in a mirror, but rather we gave ourselves the freedom to trust that God had created each of us uniquely. And in our respect for the diversity came greater unity.

As I became more conscious of the importance of relationships, the *need* for a job—the personal and often self-absorbed demands for status, ego building, and title—became less and less important. Slowly I began to see that a job, if it was to be anything at all, must be an opportunity for me to give myself away in caring relationships rather than simply be a filling station for a deflated self-esteem. In a way, I had written in my mind a job description for ministry.

And grace breeds grace.

Just as I began to wrestle with whether I should stay at home or take a job, a strange thing happened. After writing "We Can Cope" for the American Cancer Society, I met with Judy MacKintosh, a social worker at University Hospital of Cleveland's Ireland Cancer Center, who was interested in music therapy. Judy, who had led the "I Can Cope" cancer support group I had attended, arranged for me to present a program on music therapy for social workers and nurses at the hospital. During the forty-five-minute meeting, they became enamored with the idea. One of the nurses, Rosalee Tyner Anderson, wrote a formal letter to Dr. Hillard Lazarus, head of the bone marrow transplant unit, requesting music therapy on the unit. After speaking with me personally, Dr. Lazarus requested a small grant from the American Cancer Society for a feasibility study. It took more than a gentle bit of persuasion by Russell Catanese, director of the Cuyahoga County branch of the ACS, but a $2,000 grant was approved, mainly for instruments. The study started in November 1984. When I look back, I see what a difference was made when each of those people spoke up at an appropriate moment—Judy, then Rosalee, Dr. Lazarus, and Russell.

About six months into the program, I learned that Dr. Nathan Berger wanted to see me. To be honest, I didn't even know who the man was. I soon learned that he was the director of the Ireland Cancer Center. His secretary told me, "When you come in to see Dr. Berger, bring your credentials." I asked her if I had done something wrong, something inappropriate; she did not respond, except to set up a date and time.

I walked to Dr. Berger's office down a long corridor, through a door on the right, and then even farther back. It felt, every step of it, like a walk to the woodshed. Dr. Berger, a large man with a large desk, was shuffling papers as I walked in. I sat down in the only other chair and folded my hands over the paperwork in my lap. He looked up as if he were coming up for air and reoriented himself.

"Young lady," he began in a serious tone, "I've heard about your music therapy." As he talked, he measured each word as carefully as a pharmacist might weigh a powdered drug. "The patients tell me that you sing to them." A long pause. "They say that they feel better." Another pause. "They tell me that you get the staff involved." Another pause. In his slow, meticulous, and careful manner, the man was a master of intrigue; I was nearly bursting with suspense. What was he getting at? "I get letters from some of the family members telling me how much they appreciate what you do." *The punch line*, I found myself thinking, *please, get to the punch line.* And then, from out of the blue, he delivered his final line with perfect timing, "I have just two questions for you, young lady," he stated in a monotone. "When do you want to come to work for us, and how much money do you want?"

I stammered a bit—something about a childhood dream—and finally said, "I'd love to give it a try." He came up with an hourly wage (beyond my wildest dreams) and suggested that I work sixteen hours a week. He made it clear to me that this would work on a trial basis, but he would give me his full support. That was it. With the same tone in his voice, he dismissed me.

In the expected order of things, this was pure grace. On the surface I felt the irony: a measured and dignified middle-aged Jewish man, firmly committed to science and correct e-nun-ci-a-tion, giving a young, highly enthusiastic, chattering black woman with a song and dance and no firm proof a job in a prestigious hospital. And this at a time when the medical profession was incredibly suspicious of anything that might be even remotely mistaken for warm-and-fuzzy. It certainly violated no laws, either physical or social, but who would have ever imagined such a thing? I later learned, as a friendship developed with Dr. Berger, that he had played guitar during his college years, sometimes earning tuition money by playing in bars. He was in a unique way open to and grateful for music's unexpected powers.

The job offer complicated our family life. In September 1985, I had enrolled in a doctoral program at Case Western Reserve; I was also working three days a week at the Raub Developmental Center. If I took the job at Ireland Cancer Center, I would be working an additional sixteen hours a week. I was, to understate the issue, concerned about the pace of life and the effects it would have on our family.

The job offer came at a time when I was struggling with the idea of roles. Should I stay home and be a full-time mother, or did God want me to use my gifts in different ways also? As I looked back, I realized that the transitions I had gone through had been smooth ones, that Ernest and I had been eased into my career. For example, after the internship for my music therapy degree in 1979, I took a summer job working in a school for behaviorally disturbed children. Because it was temporary, it was an easy job to accept. Then following immediately on the heels of that job came the offer to work at the Raub Developmental Center. We did not have much time to think about it. At the time Martin was seven and in school full time; Curtis had not yet been born. Our next-door neighbor, Mary Long, who had two children of her own, took care of Martin a short time in the morning and an hour in the afternoon.

After Curtis was born in October 1981, I continued to work at the Raub Center, but I decreased my schedule to only three days a week. A lovely mother-daughter family, Edith and Carrie Riley, took, loved, and nurtured Curtis while I was working, making it easier for Ernest and me to deal with my work.

Although life was hectic and the laundry was sometimes left undone, we managed. As I considered these past transitions, I realized we had had only a few crises, one of which sticks in my mind to this day. During one of my last years at Raub, Martin, who never got sick, had to stay home from school with a sore throat and a low-grade fever. He was about ten years old at the time. Ernest had a big meeting that day and couldn't stay with him. I had scheduled a concert at a nursing home with my sing-and-sign choir; the bus had been paid for; the residents were expecting us; invitations had been sent out; the press had been called. I couldn't find a baby-sitter on such short notice. I didn't know what to do. Finally, I chose to leave Martin by himself for a couple of hours. It all worked out well—Martin slept while I was gone—but the experience left me feeling dirty, sick at heart for having to choose between our son and my job. I knew in my heart that I had made the wrong decision. It frightened me. I remember that Ernest and I had a long talk about my priorities—which came first, my job or our family?

In my mind, I have never doubted the answer. When it comes to roles, I am first and foremost committed to our family. I have always been enmeshed in the high calling of being a mother and a wife. Very few things in life have the potential to make a greater impact on the world. At the same time I believed that God had gifted me in unique ways to serve outside the immediate boundaries of family. As I attached less value on what the job could do for me and more on what I could do for others, I began to experience the wider range of impact I could have to love my neighbor.

But in that fall of 1985, the transitions were no longer so easy, and a harder reality fell on Ernest and me. Could I work two part-time jobs, continue to pursue my doctorate, and still be a good or even adequate mother and wife? I wish I could tell you that it was an easy decision; it most certainly was not. In fact, Ernest and I have not always agreed about this area of our life. Yet my bout with cancer again had taught us a valuable lesson: much of life is not either black or white. To grow and love, we must wrestle with the gray areas of uncertainty. Outside of order—biblical command as well as natural, physical, or moral laws—the world often gets messy. In some ways it would be much easier to hide behind stereotypes, assumptions, molds, and preconceptions, than to deal with the trauma of difficult decisions. But the cancer had taught us this: pain should never be a reason in itself to avoid dealing with life. It is in the gray areas of life where our faith, as well as the potential for growth, is most apparent. So we wrestled, and to this day we wrestle.

I often overdo it. From the fall of 1985 to the fall of 1986, I worked two days a week at Ireland Cancer Center, three days a week at the Raub Center, and continued my doctoral work. In the fall of 1986, I quit my job at Raub and began a year of residency for my doctorate. I continued to work sixteen hours a week at Ireland. Following my year of residency, I accepted a full-time position at Ireland, which eventually expanded to include other areas of University Hospitals of Cleveland, including Rainbow Babies and Children's Hospital. In 1991, I completed my doctorate in music education.

Before taking the job at Ireland in 1987, I didn't know what I was in for. Quite frankly, things have often been crazy. Late into the night I would study under a book light. Early in the morning I found myself trying to find a sock that the washer had eaten. After I had come home from work I would remember I had forgotten to pick up eggs. Weekends were especially hectic as I tried to make up for all the things I had left undone during the week: ironing, cleaning, buying groceries, attacking menacing piles of laundry, shopping, preparing for Sunday school and church. That was in addition to choir rehearsals, Sunday school lessons, church youth activities, and social outings. Our lives were on a continual treadmill, and we moved from exhilaration to exhaustion. We simply had no time to relax, talk, think, read, or do something just for the fun of it.

When we as a family battled, it was almost always about

priorities. And back then we simply had none, or we were simply too tired to rummage through our thoughts to find them. We lived our lives in the light-headed ozone of the urgent.

Over the years we have tried consciously to establish and live with priorities. We have realized that we don't have to do everything. For example, if all of one's life is given over to God, why is it necessary to be a part of every church ministry, even if I happen to be the most qualified person to lead, say, the church choir? Do our children *need* to be in every computer club, soccer league, drama, and 4-H group in the county? Can we afford *not* to take the time away together, just Ernest and me, for a romantic weekend? Is doing *something* always more profitable than doing absolutely nothing at all? And what a word—*profitable*. What exactly does that mean?

Unfortunately our lives are still often far too fast-paced. Yet with conscious effort, we are trying to restore some order through the laying down of laws and priorities in the creeping chaos.

Failing that, I sometimes look back to a time when I wondered if I would have *any* more time in my life, when I wondered if the chaos of cancer would give me the order, the grace of another day.

Just as theology moves out of chaos into law and grace, empiricism moves from information to science and art, and practicality moves out of what we might believe into proof and transcendence, so music moves out of the dissonance of endless notes and emerges in the laws of chords, harmonies, intervals. Then either beyond or through the order leaps the surprise of the unexpected: the way an occasional high A note lingers, stirs, transforms, suspends reality. I knew all of that.

But I was entering a world dominated by science, inflexible laws, and the demand of data. As I started my part-time job at Ireland Cancer Center in 1987, I managed to resurrect a few fears. Could I do this? Could I prove myself in a scientific arena where proof was the bottom line? Was I smart enough or equipped enough or measured enough? From the first day I was aware of the irony: a medically untrained woman with, say, a tambourine in a world of magnetic resonance, tomography, and hyperalimentations. In the machinery of efficiency, of what possible use is a rendition of "You Light Up My Life," no matter how stirring?

Others were also aware of the contrast. One day the hospital elevator became a place that invoked titles and the pecking order. A young, white-coated doctor stood beside me in the elevator. As I looked straight ahead, I could feel him eyeing my nametag: Deforia Lane, Music Therapist. I knew that he was turning that over in his head. Finally, apparently comfortable with his position, he asked a series of questions: "Music therapist? What will they think of next? What do you do, drop the needle on the record player?"

Not everyone was that blatant with their intellectual ignorance. But in 1985, hospitals were dominated by technology, data, tests, charted results. In my effort to be accepted, I found myself at times losing balance: I focused on the science of music therapy. I relied on learned techniques. I assessed, analyzed, applied, monitored, measured, and evaluated.

I spouted data whenever I could. Facts, like bullets. Studies showed or suggested that music can

- reduce blood pressure and heart and respiration rates;
- decrease pain perception, levels of fear, stress, and anxiety;
- increase feelings of self-worth and reduce depression;
- occupy some of the brain's neurological pathways and reduce the number of neurotransmitters that are available to transmit pain messages;
- reduce feelings of helplessness by giving the patient a sense of control in a setting that is often depersonalizing.

I quoted Beck, who supported using music therapy as an intervention to relieve cancer pain, and Guzetta, who demonstrated positive effects of music in a coronary unit, and Updike, who showed that music produces desirable shifts in physiological and emotional states of patients before surgery.

I spouted the results of studies.

- At California State University in Fresno a psychologist studied thirty migraine-headache sufferers for five weeks. Some of the patients listened to their favorite music; others used relaxation or biofeedback techniques; a control group did neither. All three groups received similar medications. The results: music proved the most effective supplemental technique. A year later patients who continued to listen to music reported 83 percent fewer headaches.

- Clinical researchers at the Georgia Baptist Medical Center in Atlanta discovered that premature or low-weight babies gained weight faster and used oxygen more efficiently when they listened to music. Babies exposed to an hour-and-a-half of music each day averaged only eleven days in the intensive care unit, compared with sixteen days for control groups.

- After classical music was provided in critical care units at Baltimore's St. Agnes Hospital, the need for medicine to control pain or anxiety decreased dramatically. Said one doctor, "Half an hour of music produced the same effect as ten milligrams of Valium." Also patients who had not been able to sleep, some for as long as three to four days, fell into a deep sleep after listening to music.

I could explain how the human body processes music. For example, I could quote Harvey: "Sound vibrations are channeled through the ear as well as skin and bone conduction and are processed in the brain stem (reticular activating system), and neural impulses trigger autonomic nervous system reactions, which in turn produce changes in respiration, pulse rate, blood pressure, muscle tone, brainwave frequency, galvanic skin response, pilomotor reflexes, pupilary reflexes, gastric motility. . . ."

145

I could speak as well on the proven behavioral effects of this physiological process:

- music can move through the auditory cortex directly to the limbic system, the regulating center of emotional response;
- music can trigger strong emotions, which affect the autonomic nervous system, which releases certain hormones and endorphins, the body's natural painkillers;
- music, when played at a moderate tempo over the speakers of a supermarket store, accounted for a 28 percent increase in the purchase of groceries (people walked in rhythm with the slower pace of music, thereby having more time to pick up more items);
- tempo of music can affect sexual drive; a frenzied tempo and blaring metal guitars can physically excite the genitals.

While writing my dissertation, which I completed in 1991, I conducted my own research. I tested the relationship between music and the release of salivary immunoglobulin A (IgA), an antibody in saliva that helps prevent bacteria from entering the digestive and respiratory tracts. The average person in good health has a sufficient level of IgA, but during an illness the level is reduced or drops off completely, leaving the patient susceptible to infection.

To determine if one individual music-therapy session could measurably affect IgA, we took forty hospitalized patients with varying diagnoses and randomly put them in either an experimental group or a control group. The twenty patients in the experimental group were given thirty minutes of individual music therapy, while the others were allowed to continue in the normal hospital routine. Pre- and post-therapy samples of saliva were taken from both groups. Results demonstrated that the subjects that received music therapy had a significant increase in salivary IgA, with a p=>.01 value.

If people wanted science, data, facts, results, and studies, I was prepared. I knew that music had its own laws and dynamics that could be charted, documented, proven, and tested. Music therapy, I knew, was not just a touchy-feely-mushy abstract theory but a technique anchored in concrete, scientific fact. Among doctors, nurses, and health-care specialists, I desired some respect. But almost no one asked me for the data, the proof that music therapy worked, not even Dr. Berger, the director of Ireland Cancer Center.

I wanted to approach my patients with techniques learned through nine years of graduate, postgraduate, and now doctoral education. Yet as I looked at my new job, I came to a frightening realization: very few of my learned techniques applied to my current situation. At Raub Developmental Center, for example, I worked primarily through reinforcement. I would try to get a severely retarded child to move from one goal to the next through positive reinforcement of music. I could measure behavioral change with any number of techniques. During a certain period of time, I could count the number of times a person banged his head on a wall or threw himself to the floor or peed in his diaper. I was working, for the most part, with a focus of specific behavioral changes.

But in the hospital environment at Ireland Cancer Center, my focus was markedly different. The people with whom I was working were fully developed and intelligent. They hardly needed or wanted to be rewarded by my allowing them to bang on a drum, blow into a kazoo, or eat a raisin. I was, in many senses, making it up as I went along.

Even so, I attempted as best I could to stay within the confines of science, technique, and measurable results. In fact, one of the objectives of the grant from the American Cancer Society was to measure the effects of music on heart rate, blood pressure, and pain perception. I was to keep accurate records. But it didn't take long to see the hitch in this plan. Because I didn't know how to monitor heart rates and blood pressures, I had to rely on a nurse to take these measurements. However, I could never get the service of a nurse at the right time. If measurements were not taken immediately, they would not reflect the effects of the music.

I also had problems integrating highly technical medical information into my therapy. As I met each week with the team of doctors, nurses, and specialists to discuss patient care, I was confused and intimidated. Although I understood some of what the doctors hoped to see—movement, more fluid intake, lessening of depression—I couldn't begin to understand the jargon: double STO, cut APG, anaphylaxis, cyclosporin, hematocrit, palliative measures, veno-occlusive diseases. . . . In the dazed look that covered my face, I nourished my worst fear: my attempt at music therapy could jeopardize someone's health.

In those early days and weeks, I also remember some frustration in working with patients. Twenty-four-year-old Gail, for example, had come to the hospital to have a baby, but in some of the testing related to her delivery, the doctors discovered she had leukemia. I went to her with my procedures, a list of options:

- use cassette tapes for relaxing or energizing the body;
- use music before, during, and after surgery and painful procedures;
- schedule music-therapy sessions during family visits;
- develop a musical skill on an instrument;
- compose lyrics or instrumental music to reflect inner thoughts and feelings;
- develop a personalized visualization tape;
- have the music therapist sing or play songs of her choice.

But Gail wanted none of these options. Where should I go with her? We talked. We talked about her children, about the music she liked, about her rabble-rousing days and her street-tough ways, and about what she wanted out of her life.

Gradually it hit me: people weren't interested in participating in another scientific study. They were tired of being treated for what they *had* and not for who they *were*. The excess of science that I was trying to squeeze into music therapy—the monitoring, data keeping, techniques—was exactly what the patients didn't want and what I knew almost instinctively they didn't need. While I was wrestling with how I could make music therapy more competent, verifiable, and valid, the patients were often searching for a hand to hold or a simple song to sing.

Humor, I have come to understand, is one of God's most gentle and corrective measures. In my desire to appear professional, scientific, and competent, God brought into my life people and circumstances that served as parody.

One of my first patients was Terry, who was about to have a bone-marrow transplant. Because of anxiety and loneliness, he was having trouble sleeping. One of the nurses suggested that I could "play something soft for him." I went in with my spiel: what music therapy is, what it could do, and the list of options. More than anything, Terry wanted someone with whom he could talk. He later told me that when I entered his room, he had been praying that God would bring him someone to help with his loneliness.

Feeling a camaraderie with me, Terry responded to music. I found out that he loved to sing hymns, and one day he decided to sing "Oh, How I Love Jesus." To do so, he had to remove his oxygen mask. When the nurse came in, she was taken aback. She started to cry when she saw his strength and deep emotion. For a few moments Terry had transcended his disease and had moved on. The whole atmosphere had changed, and people noticed.

The nurse then took his blood pressure. "Good grief, this is the lowest I've ever seen it." Word started to spread among the nurses about music therapy.

To help with Terry's insomnia, I suggested that he listen to music on a cassette player. Since Terry didn't have a player of his own, I brought my husband's tape player in the next day.

"Try this," I told him, "and see if it helps. I'm going to see another patient. I'll come back in about twenty minutes to see how you are doing." When I returned, he was fast asleep, snoring loudly.

Although I was pleased that the music helped so dramatically, I also had a problem. The tape player that he was listening to was my huband's. How was I going to get it back? Talk about your tests of professionalism. I stood there trying to decide which of the following options would be appropriate: (a) let him sleep and keep the tape recorder for awhile, even though my husband might need it; (b) walk up to him, carefully remove the headphones and gently pry his fingers off the tape player; (c) continue to stand there awkwardly watching him snore.

For the longest time, I selected (c): stand there and watch him snore. Finally, I made a series of noises—a cough, a rustle of papers, a tapping of fingers—each increasing in volume. Finally, he awoke. I think I may have bought him his own tape player.

Then there was the time I witnessed my first bone-marrow aspiration, a painful procedure done while the patient is conscious. The patient, a woman in her twenties, had not done well when she had had similar procedures done earlier. Although drugs help deaden the pain, they do not take it all away. I suggested that music might further help reduce the pain. Through headphones, she listened to her favorite music.

She did just fine. I was the one who suffered distress. Samples of marrow are extracted by cutting a hole in the bone with what appeared to be a hand drill. In this particular case, the doctor was having a difficult time getting deep enough into the bone. He would drill, bring it back out, and then insert a syringe into the hole to draw the marrow, which looks like thick blood. Each time, though, he would come up empty and would have to continue the drilling, applying more and more pressure until nearly all his weight was leveraged onto the drill. I still remember the sound of the steel and bone. I noticed that I was starting to see little stars. I thought it was a hot flash. I didn't even have time to catch myself on the way down. A nurse, noticing that I was passing out, told an intern who was standing next to me, "Would you get her, please?" It was the first and only time that I have passed out.

Eventually I began to relax. Part of it was that I began to understand the punch lines. Part of it was that, despite my overemphasis on technique, the music was having a powerful influence, in some cases quite dramatically. And part of it was the recognition that music, even though it is saturated in law and order, has a unique power to transcend a given reality. As I settled on a better balance between science and art, technique and tenderness, I soon discovered that I was unleashing the real power in music, a connection that no scalpel or drug could ever reach. In the sameness of the science around me, the uniqueness of music—the art—began to break through.

Sometimes I surprised even myself. At the end of each team meeting, the nurse would ask if anyone had further questions. One day I started talking: "Mr. Robinson, who has been with us some time, is going home today; I think it would be nice if we all would sing him a discharge song; I am handing out copies of a song I have composed for the occasion. Choose one instrument to play, and we'll go over the song once and sing it; it shouldn't take much time at all."

My speech, I am certain, was compressed into one breath, for I feared if I took any time to pause, I would either lose my courage or be cut off. After I finished, the room was dead quiet. Here were these doctors, specialists, and nurses, all highly educated, trained and competent, staring at a maraca or handbell or triangle. Suspense hung in the silence. How would they respond? Would it be below their dignity? Was this a brash move destined to end in failure?

Finally one of the nurses chuckled as she read one of the verses. From the other side of the table, a doctor began to shake a tambourine. Then, one by one, like a group of four-year-olds, they began to play, rattle, shake, and drum. "Okay," I said, taking advantage of momentum. "Here's the pitch, ummmmmm."

In the end this group of health-care specialists descended on Mr. Robinson's room to sing him this song:

> (*Sung to the tune of "Rinky-Dinky Parlez-Vous"*)
> Who's leaving this hospital room today?
> Mr. Robinson.
> Who learned two instruments to play?
> Mr. Robinson.
> Who kept a positive attitude but couldn't stomach this
>   hospital food?
> That's our Freddy Robinson.
> Who talked on the phone and splashed on cologne?
> Mr. Robinson.
> Who rode on the bike and slept through each night?
> Mr. Robinson.
> The nurses and docs say, "Keep healthy and sound."
> It's true you can't keep a good man down.
> Mr. Freddy Robinson.

On the third floor of the Ireland Cancer Center, amid all the science and technology and jargon, floated the notes of a song, sung off-key. For me, the music was pure and sweet. It sounded just like laughter.

The magic, I suspected, had just begun. In the laws of science, what was unexpected moved exactly like grace.

Chapter Nine

Faith, Hope and Love:
Three Stories

And now these three remain: faith, hope and love.
—1 Corinthians 13:13a

Faith, Hope, and Love: Three Stories

Con spirito (with spirit)

Faith

The blind date, if it would have been between anyone other than George and Carolyn, may have never happened. George's car battery died. When he called Carolyn, whom he had met through a friend, and asked her if she would mind driving, she thought that only a little strange and went to pick him up.

That was the beginning, back in 1960; he was twenty-six, she was twenty-one. A few months later, George happened to mention that he thought that they should stop dating other people, and he, for one, would not be surprised if they were engaged soon. That was in March 1961. Just five months later, they were married.

For nearly the next thirty years, that's the way it was with George and Carolyn. They sensed by some odd instinct what the other lacked or wanted or was trying to say. It was communication stripped to its barest elements—without loud announcements, without the need for great events, and without, in many cases, the fanfare of precise words. They just loved each other.

Both of their lives were marked by a sense of continuity and a movement of tradition. That was, to some degree, part of their compatibility. They came from identical families: their fathers were doctors, their mothers were nurses, and they both had three siblings. And like their families, George and Carolyn both sought to give to their own four children the best that life had to offer: art, faith, education, music, examples of loving relationships.

More times than not, they rose to the top. In a very real sense, they just couldn't help it.

I met Carolyn in 1989, during the final phases of her struggle with cancer. She struck me immediately as a person graced with grace. Even while waging a fierce battle, she was composed, intense, warm, honest. I never, not even once, saw her buckle under the weight of cancer.

I have chosen to write about Carolyn not because of some spectacular event that took place between us. We shared music by talking about the orchestral classics. I would sing to her sometimes, hymns or music from the theater, maybe, "On a Clear Day." Music did not bring her out of a coma. We shared no profound conversations about the meaning of life. She cried only when she had to. In fact, no single event or circumstance in Carolyn's story stands out as remarkable.

She was spectacular, in the end, because she was so unspectacular. Consistent in the day-to-day grinds of faith, love, and patience, she was always looking for the next small step in her quest for that distant star.

Carolyn always seemed to stay in control. Through chemotherapy, through the pain, through the loss of ability to do certain things, she remained together, as if some emotional glue held her together.

To the very end, she was a planner. A year earlier, when her cancer's symptoms first started to reappear, she had planned her daughter's entire wedding. She planned ways to beat her cancer. She read books about her cancer. She studied the connections between the mind and body. She worked hard, in whatever things were left to her, at getting well.

And through it all, in the accumulation of everyday decisions, she maintained a balance that stunned me. Until the end, she gave of herself.

But that was Carolyn. It was in the everyday, little decisions that she left her legacy of greatness. Until her youngest child was thirteen, she stayed at home with her four children. She knew that was where she was most needed. She provided the children with all the tools they needed, but more than that she gave them her presence, that always safer reality that she was there for them. She knew that was necessary.

When the children grew older, she decided to return to school. She earned her bachelor's degree from Cleveland State University in 1980. Two years later, she was awarded a master's degree in speech pathology, also from Cleveland State University, where she was awarded the Outstanding Speech Pathology graduate award. Through her own efforts, she began working with patients from hospitals and private practices. Both her colleagues and her patients loved and respected her.

Yet success, whether at home or in business, did not change Carolyn. She lived in a world of debutantes and cotillions and high society with humility and laughter, just as she had when she had been a young girl. She was cultured, hinting of the Ivy League, without being pretentious. She was never in awe of herself or her family. She remained balanced.

But it was more than just a disciplined sort of grace. It was in some sense a part of who Carolyn was. She radiated a kind of attractiveness, a sense of composition or magnetism. At her memorial service, her brother, Bill, spoke of the peace Carolyn had radiated to him as a young child. He remembered one night during World War II, when the sky over their house was full of planes. He and Carolyn sat in their bedroom, looking out of their window, wondering if their town would be bombed. Bill said that although he was afraid, Carolyn, even without speaking a word, calmed him. Her presence alone drove away fear.

Even after the cancer exploded within her, she still found a way of radiating a peace that was beyond words. Within herself, she balanced the tension of such conflicting emotions. Just before Carolyn died, I wrote her a letter. It read, in part:

"You have taught me much about living. How to smile and be gracious in the face of adversity. That it is possible to be realistic and not morbid, that it is possible to possess hope without entertaining denial, and that tears are as natural and permissible as laughter. I have observed with awe your tenderness toward your family, how you nurture and undergird them and protect them from hurt as much as is humanly possible. I have looked on the heavy heart of your husband and sensed his grief but have equally felt his abounding love for you and his determination to make each day with you count.

"It is not my intent to glamorize these past few months of your life but rather to make you aware of how your character, carriage, and coping have been perceived through my eyes. You have a rare and sterling quality about you. It has not succumbed to the intensity of pressure or crumbled under the rigors of your circumstances. You face your down days and prepare to get the most out of the good ones. And you have a way of complimenting your caregivers and making us feel that *we* are the ones who deserve the praise."

As the cancer progressed, George and Carolyn were able to take trips together. In keeping with who they were, the trips were nothing spectacular. Some were just a hop in the car and a drive west into the sunset. Others were a lunch on the public square where one of their sons was playing in a band. Or still others were an evening of classical music at a nearby outdoor music pavilion. On their last vacation together, to Hilton Head, South Carolina, people would have never even guessed that she was sick. They went with their best friends, ate late dinners at seafood restaurants, walked the beach, sometimes past midnight. She would tire easily, but after rest, she would be ready for more.

Carolyn's concerns about her cancer were mainly about George and their children. She worried about how they were coping, and how they would cope after she died. She was always thinking of others.

And making plans. Even before she had become sick, Carolyn and George had decided that they would be cremated and buried at Lakewood Park. George had made an arrangement to buy a certain niche inside a mausoleum. Carolyn wanted to go and pick out where she was to be. The interior was done in a Williamsburg style. George and Carolyn sat in two wing chairs and looked around. Carolyn chose her niche, about eye level, in bronze. They sat some more, sometimes talking and sometimes not. They both commented on how quiet it was, how still. And even here, in the Williamsburg blue of death, George couldn't help but sensing the peace that his wife radiated.

As I came to know and understand Carolyn better, I began to see that it was not Carolyn who was in control. She had her weaknesses, many of them in fact. It was Carolyn's faith that stabilized her. She was so balanced because God centered her. Two of her favorite verses, both of which were read at her funeral, came from Romans 8:28, 38–39. "And we know that in all things God works for the good of those who love him, who have been called according to his purpose.... For I am convinced that neither death nor life, neither angels nor demons, neither the present nor the future, nor any powers, neither height nor depth, nor anything else in all creation, will be able to separate us from the love of God that is in Christ Jesus our Lord."

This was her faith. She knew in the everyday decisions of life what true success was. In some random notes she left in a book she was reading before she died, she wrote: "I learn to live out of my weaknesses, not my strengths. Success in situations is not to move out of a situation but to move God into the situation."

At her funeral, I sang a song that we had composed together.

I have always been one who loves growing,
Reaching for that distant star.
Finding the strength that sustains me in life
Can be your strength wherever you are,

Wherever you are.
Life is full of such treasure, full of such grace:
Choices, decisions, in all that you face.
Lend me your ear and together we'll share,
For life has such meaning when people care.

Hope

Samantha, that was the name your mother chose. She liked it for no particular reason, no deeper significance than the music in its consonants, the way they slow-danced, like rain, on her tongue. But the music in a thing—a name, a song, the rhythm in a horse trot—was of no small consequence. Samantha. That was your name, provided you were a girl, of course, just three months into your mother's womb.

I am not sure, Samantha, if your mother knew the meaning of your name, the one that the librarian would give if you were old enough to ask. Your grandmother doesn't know, for sure. Your father, he is keeping awfully busy. And your mother . . . well, let's talk of this later.

Listener, that is what your name means. I like your name, but I naturally would; without listeners, music therapists would simply be out of a job. If you are faithful to your name, little one, you will know the joys of listening: music, a thunderstorm over the bay, a train in the distance, the eruption of spring. Your mother, what little I know of her, was a listener. Her mother—your precious and strong-willed grandmother—told me once that she could play the piano by ear. Once at a very early age, she was pulled out of her normal school class to demonstrate and practice her gift. That may not sound like much, Samantha, but it is. Your mother could hear the ring in an August morning rain, the music in a child's laugh, the movement in her baby girl's name.

I wish I could have known your mother, Samantha, I mean beyond the three-by-five, faded color photograph that hung above her hospital bed: the shoulder-length red hair, the button nose, broad smile. Twenty is an age steeped in energy. I wish that you could know your mother, now that you are outside the womb, in this troublesome, beautiful, fierce world into which you have been born.

But your mom, little one, is gone. I know this may sound strange to you, but you were alive in your mother's womb when she technically was already dead. I must make this simpler: your mother's brain was considered dead, but her body remained alive. She hung on in some mysterious way so that you might live, so that you might be able to listen.

After they brought your mom to the hospital where I work, she "lived" for only twenty minutes. To the best of our knowledge, the pain medicine that she was taking for injuries she suffered a year earlier in a car accident caused her to bleed into her brain. Her body, and you nearly six months inside her womb, were kept alive through machines that nourished her with food, water, and oxygen.

We knew that music would be important to you. It was not only in your name but also in your genes. Your mother, you know, had a gift for music, could hear it on the radio and in everyday things. Your father loved songs too. He was a drummer in a band, beating out the rhythms of a once-troubled life. Together your parents found a certain harmony. And you, Samantha, the child of this union, would surely appreciate music, especially in this room of whirs and beeps and alarms and electronic monitors—your mother's forced breathing. I came to play and sing for you.

That was when I met you, Samantha. I'll have to admit that I was afraid to come see you at first. As a music therapist, I had never been asked to give the gift of music to an unborn child, especially through the body of a brain-dead mother. I made myself, one leg after the other, walk into your hospital room: my feet were like lead, my heart like melted wax. Forgive me, Samantha, if I found myself feeling my way through this. I placed my Omnichord on automatic pilot by your side, centered my hands on your mother's abdomen, and began to sing:

He's got the whole world in his hands;
He's got the whole world in his hands;
He's got the whole world in his hands;
He's got the whole world in his hands.

I didn't expect that you would understand, what with being inside a dead mother's womb, but I wanted to let you know that you were loved. I wanted you to feel it, a song rippling through your warm, dark world.

You, in God's hands, underneath my fingers, caressed by music slow and gliding, danced. We sang other songs for you: "This Old Man" and "Samantha Had a Little Lamb." You listened and moved. The faster I sang and played, the faster you moved. Once when a nurse was playing fast music, your heartbeat raced so fast that we had to stop the song. Your father sang to you sometimes too. He tried to be joyful, but I could tell he was in pain, reeling in the contradiction that was always before his eyes. He told me of how he and your mom had met each other just a year earlier. He told me of their dates: hiking, fishing, swimming, and riding horses. He also told me of how he sometimes would catch himself singing for no apparent reason. Forgive him, Samantha, if he just didn't feel like singing right now.

Your grandmother also sang to you. I knew that she would be the one who would take care of you; I wanted you to become familiar with her voice. I thought of taping your grandmother singing nursery rhymes and children's lullabies, so that when we were gone from your mother's room, we could wrap the headphones around her tight belly so that you could hear your grandmother's voice.

For nearly six weeks we sang, played, laughed, and cried as we awaited your arrival, little one. Your approaching birth signaled such a paradox of life and death, treasure and tragedy, laughter and tears, celebration and memorial, da capo and fine. There you were, in the middle of a room of machines, in the womb of a mother who would never know you, and you were moving and dancing, and in the music, listening. Who could explain such a kicking of hope in an otherwise graceless room?

Just before you were born, Samantha, we held a memorial service in the hospital room for your mother. Your great-grandparents, your grandmother, two nurses, a doctor, and a chaplain were there. We heard of your mother's dreams. Out of boredom more than anything else, she had dropped out of high school when she had been a sophomore. Realizing the importance of getting an education, she began studying to earn her high school equivalency degree. In 1992, just two years before you were born, she failed her exam by just two-thirds of one point. She was crushed, but she continued to study. She had plans to take the test again in the spring. We also heard of her excitement when she found out about you, how she ran around, screaming with joy. She talked all the time about seeing you. She had high hopes.

Your birthday, Samantha, was your mother's last day.

Doctors, nurses, surgeons, anesthesiologists, and pediatricians were marked in teams by scrubs of green, light blue, and rose. Soon after you were delivered by Cesarean section, the doctors, at your mother's request, took her kidneys, pancreas, liver, and heart. Your mother knew that people waited desperately for such gifts. On your birthday, your mother gave life to more than just you.

This drama of life and death included a carefully scripted and timed protocol. All the possibilities had been considered, planned for, anticipated. Nothing was left to chance. In a room of beige and gray, windowless and artificially bright, the buzz of anticipation was flat, calculated, yet unmistakably colored by a rainbow of emotion. They were not sure, Samantha, about how well you might do in a world such as this.

But I have hope for you. I know that you dance with such grace. I know how the music stirs you, moves you, even when death surrounded you. I have felt you under my fingers, in the time of a song, poking, rolling, somersaulting, kicking.

In the waiting room of the intensive-care nursery, your grandmother longed to see your face, to hold you in her arms.

In the releasing of her daughter to death, her hope was in you. In her mind the song of life goes on; at the moment of her daughter's death, she regained a piece of her in you, the first-born of her firstborn. Along with your grandmother waited your thirteen-year-old aunt, Jennifer, who will be for all practical purposes your sister.

It then was time. The surgeon, through the cut in your mother's womb, fished for you, searching for just the correct grasp. Fifteen seconds seem like an eternity; everyone waited in silence. And then with one quick movement of the surgeon's hand, you were here: dripping wet, trailing a long cord, tiny fingers, toes, round head, eyes closed, one with beauty.

You made just one tiny squeak: a pink, healthy cry of distress. To me, it sounded like music.

A short time after your birth, Samantha, they held a funeral for your mother. Friends and relatives gave testimony to the courage, the hope, and the dreams of a twenty-year-old woman, who had died too young. They talked about the miracle that, even in the tragedy of such a young death, she could bring forth such life. They cried, laughed, and sang. But for your grandmother who now cradles you in her arm and sings you to sleep each night, that was not the best of it. This was: when they flashed a slide of your mother, as an infant, on a projection screen, your grandmother could have sworn it was you, Samantha.

Are you still listening, little one? Then hear this: you are loved.

Love

I met Brad in room 6073, a corner room of the sixth floor in Ireland Cancer Center. His wife, Beverly, was standing near a window in the room. Jason, Brad's sandy-haired ten-year-old son, was also there. Brad's cancer, non-Hodgkin's lymphoma, had metastasized to his brain. This was 1987.

Fifteen years earlier, in 1972, Brad and Beverly had fallen

in love; they had both worked in the same hospital, he as an accountant, she in medical records. She started sitting at a table behind him. One day he turned around and asked her if he could join her. She said she knew in an instant that this was the person she would marry. He had felt the same thing.

No one could have guessed it. They were so different from one another. He was athletic, calm, funny, businesslike when he had to be, Catholic; she was slightly flighty, quiet, a woman who might look over her shoulder, Protestant. But they clicked. For their first date, they went to a restaurant in Sandusky, Ohio, a quaint French number, the Mon Ami. He didn't tell her then about the boat or the cottage; he didn't want her to like him for his things.

He, the former president of the Cleveland State University Ski Club, agreed to take beginning ski lessons with Beverly because she didn't want to take classes alone. He had to pretend that he didn't know how to ski. The instructor kept telling Beverly she was doing everything right; he told Brad that he was doing everything wrong. When Brad couldn't keep from laughing anymore, he did some fancy ski moves. His secret was out.

Brad and Beverly dated for about a year. At the shore of Lake Erie, near the Enchanted Forest, considered to be the Cadillac of miniature golf courses, they sat on a park bench and watched the sky, red and orange and purple, all the impossible blends of a summer sunset. He took a box out of his pocket and opened it up. There was a certain ring in his proposal: a circle of hope.

In room 6073, I stood at Brad's bedside and explained to him that I was a music therapist. He showed no response. For the last few months, the only thing that seemed to change was the time that had passed. He had been hospitalized in January 1987. Now it was May, five months later. Day after day it was pretty much the same thing: Brad, with head drooped, sat on his bed, responding to almost nothing. Although he was technically not in a coma, the doctors said that the cancer had caused neurological damage. They would be surprised if he ever made real contact again.

Before the cancer, his wife told me, he had been so full of life. He was a player and a fighter. The first diagnosis came in 1975. In between the births of his two children, Sherry in 1974 and Jason in 1975, Brad was in the hospital for a splenectomy, liver biopsy, and chemotherapy. The cancer went into remission, only to reappear two years later. After another round of chemotherapy and radiation, the disease mysteriously went into spontaneous remission. Where the doctors had said maybe only two to three years, Brad had squeezed out twelve.

He could do that. Brad and Beverly's favorite song was "Up Where We Belong," a song about eagles soaring high, above it all. They used to sing it to each other; they related to that. Brad was a person gifted at getting the most out of life. Even though he was often weak, sick, and in pain, he would never allow himself to be deflated. She told me about the trip they had made along the east coast to Florida shortly after his diagnosis. Beverly had worried whether he would be alive when the trip was over; he wanted to find the next beach. She told me about the time she drove in the driveway and saw their children run screaming from a man in a Dracula costume; she knew it had to be Brad. She told me about the handful of mornings in their Cleveland suburb when Brad wakened their children by playing a trumpet in the driveway.

Children loved Brad; he loved children. It was hard to tell who loved whom the most. When Sherry and Jason were born, Brad was so proud that he came to the hospital dressed in a beige suit. When Sherry took ballet lessons, Brad went to every one. He would lift up Jason's head over the door, stick his own two feet under the door, and everyone would have to say, "Look, there's the tall boy." Jason always laughed.

Even when Brad was sick at home and Beverly was at work, he would take the children to the beach. He was, in a unique way, crazy about Jason. The father-son, testosterone-driven stuff: fishing in the morning, rifle care, carburetors and alternators, the pounds in a line, the gauge in a powder, the horses under the hood. They possessed the power to make each other laugh. On their vacation drive to Florida, Brad and Jason, more like two small sisters than a father and son, would sing endless ad-libbed verses to "On Top of Spaghetti." They giggled into the wee hours of the morning, until the laughter would wear them out, and Beverly would have to take over. Brad was full of life, laughter, and a cancer that took nearly everything but his spirit.

In room 6073, more time had passed. I had talked a bit with Beverly and Jason, small talk, and Brad had not moved. Sitting up, head drooped, no sign that he was even in there. I asked Beverly and Jason if they would like to sing to Brad. They both smiled and agreed. I looked at Jason and asked, "What is your dad's favorite song?"

Without hesitation, he said, "Candyman." I know I must have giggled in surprise; I did not yet know of Brad's leanings to all things loved by children. I put the Omnichord in Jason's lap, and he took right to it. "Who can take the sunrise, sprinkle it with dew? The Candyman can." As Jason sang, Brad lifted up his head and looked at him. We all were a little stunned, but Jason had the presence to keep singing, "Who can. . . ? Oh, the Candyman can. . . ."

After Jason finished singing, I leaned over Brad and placed the Omnichord on his lap. I put his hand under my hand and onto the pressure-sensitive plate that plays chords. I asked Beverly what their favorite song was, and thankfully it was a song that I knew:

Who knows what tomorrow brings
In a world where few hearts survive?
All I know is the way I feel;
When it's real, it keeps me alive.
The road is long,
There are mountains
In our way,
But we climb a step every day.
Love lifts us up where we belong,
Where the eagles fly,
On a mountain high;
Love lifts us up where we belong.

About halfway through the song, I could feel movement in Brad's hand; he was strumming the Omnichord. After we finished, he pulled his hand purposefully out and over mine. Looking me straight in the eye, he said, "More music." We were only too happy to oblige.

"'Amazing Grace,'" Beverly called out.

When we had finished, Brad said, "Beautiful music." Tears were rolling down his cheeks. Brad was not one to cry. For the most part he kept things stored up inside, releasing the pressure with a laugh or a song or a prayer. He was connected, more than most, to children, music, and faith—the simple and profound gifts in life.

Music surrounded him all of his life. His family was one who sat around the piano and played and laughed and sang. He knew how to play the trumpet, saxophone, and piano. For most of his life, he played in a band. He could bring his listeners to tears of joy, or just plain tears. Like the time he was in the hospital at a meeting with a group of executives. The meeting was late in getting started, so Brad found a piano and started playing a classical piece. He couldn't even remember it all, so he had to ad-lib some, keeping everyone entertained and loose. That was Brad.

His faith was not just something he did; it came, like his music, from places deep inside him. In the same way that music could express his thoughts and emotions to others, prayer was the inarticulate speech of his heart. I often have wondered: Did Brad pray in the darkness of those final nights for one more break in the wall, one more chance to show and tell his family that he loved them? And in a mixture of faith and music, did he finally cry?

The doctors, of course, didn't believe it. After all, they had put words like *neurological damage, unresponsive, highly improbable* on Brad's chart. Brad could simply not have done what people were saying he did. Not more than an hour or so after Brad had so dramatically responded to the music, several doctors and nurses followed me to room 6073. I approached Brad's bed with a trail of white coats and long titles in my wake. "Brad, did you enjoy the music today?" I asked.

He answered plainly, "Yes." I was so happy that he responded! I asked him a few more questions, and each time Brad answered, "Yes." I was beginning to be afraid that the doctors might think it was just an unconscious or reflexive action; I wanted them to know, on this week before Easter, that Brad really had come back to life, that he had made connections with those he loved.

"Brad," I said, "you need to say anything but yes."

Big as day and quick as a flash, Brad said, "Anything."

That was Brad. And, make no mistake about it, he was back.

But not for long. Within a few days, he slipped back into a nonresponsive state. A few weeks later, he died. Months and years later, Beverly and Jason still visit his grave. (It would take years for Sherry, perhaps devastated the most by Brad's death, to go to the cemetery.) They would stand there, mother and son, and talk to him. "I won a speech contest, Dad. I made a great play in this baseball game against the Pirates. Sherry is dating this guy, Dad; she sings love songs in the shower."

"I did the bills today, Brad. I wish I had your skill with money. The ledger always seems to come out on the minus side. We miss you, honey."

"Remember that time, Dad, when we sang until the middle of the night? I love you, Dad. Good-bye, we'll talk to you later."

And they would wait, in silence, for him to answer.

To this day, on Brad's birthday, Jason and his mom take him a cupcake, complete with candles, and sing to him. I often wonder, *does he hear*? I can picture him in heaven, even surrounded with the grand, majestic choruses, head tilted, straining slightly, a smile on his face or tears rolling down his cheeks, saying, "Beautiful music. More music."

The music soars within the little lark,
And the lark soars.

—Elizabeth Barrett Browning

Chapter Ten

The Art of Voices

Cantando (singing)

M r. Mamie's laugh rang with music. Even with the cancer, the shortness of breath in his seventy-plus years, the fear of leaving behind his wife of five decades, he could light up the gray hospital room with his bright wit. He possessed a natural grace, a genuine kindness, and an insatiable sense of humor.

Mr. Mamie liked the idea of composing a song together. As he talked, I wrote down his thoughts so that I could put together some lyrics. When I returned to his room three days later, I knew immediately that things had changed dramatically. He was curled up on his side in bed; tubes hung from his nose. The whole room had grown somber, quiet. The shades were drawn. The half-tones of gray and silence filled the spaces once lit with the color of his laugh. It didn't seem to be the right time to sing the silly song I had composed. I walked over to the side of his bed, leaned over to whisper into his ear, and told him that I had written this song for him but that I would come back at a better time to sing it. He opened his eyes, winked, and said, "Sing it now." I felt foolish, singing this song in front of his wife, but I gave in to Mr. Mamie's request.

171

Why look on the bad side
When there's so much more to see?
Who wants a grouch sittin' slumped on a couch?
Not her! Not you! Not me!
So I'll take life as it comes;
I may need a Rolaids or a Tums.
So heads high, don't you cry,
'Cause you can't blind your eyes,
By looking on the brighter side (use Foster Grants),
By looking on the brighter side.

After I sang it, I waited for any reaction. For what seemed like the longest time, he was silent. Finally he opened both eyes real wide, called up his wildest smile, and began to sing to me: "Baby face, you've got the cutest little baby face. . . ." And that was it. Even with the little bit of energy he had left, he was able to change the atmosphere of that room. The shades went up, the sun shone in his face. Even in that broken down, unfunny body, Mr. Mamie was still the life of the party.

Some things can't be measured, charted, dissected, analyzed, formulated, calculated, or explained. Like Mr. Mamie's unsinkable laugh. How can it be that from carbon, hydrogen, oxygen, amino acid, and the other two dollars' worth of chemicals that compose the human body, arises the incalculable resiliency of the human spirit? Or, even so, is it just the air over cords of tissue, the production of vibration, or the sounding of desire, the song of a soul? Is it, then, the art of voices?

My job involves science: technique, measurement, research, calculation. My job is to solve the puzzle of the whole by the technical and competent management of the pieces. Science is all about breaking things down, a necessary movement from totality to parts. A body becomes a collection of systems, a system a collection of organs, an organ a collection of tissues, tissue a collection of cells, etc.

In music therapy, too, a song is composed of certain vibrations, which activate in the ear certain neurological responses, which trigger the release of certain hormones, which result in

172

certain types of behaviors. The therapist must diagnose each situation carefully, determine and apply the appropriate method, monitor and evaluate results, adjust treatment to reaction, and so on. Music therapy, as I have explained before, is the systematic application of music to aid in the treatment of the physiological and psychological aspects of an illness or disability.

But we must be careful in our science. With our carefully crafted definitions, equations, and dissections, we have a tendency to miss the forest for the trees; with our demands to diagnose, control, and eliminate, we often dismiss the intangible elements that mysteriously bind the parts into the whole. Call these elements what you will—soul, spirit, community, faith, hope, love—they are often at risk when our medicine becomes purely anatomical. We are, in terms of our bodies and our community, more than a simple collection of the parts.

Music repeatedly teaches me that. Was it a neurological reaction that brought Brad out of his comatose state? Certainly. But it was more than that. It was the love in his ten-year-old son's sweet, high voice. It was his wife's longing in the lyrics, "Love lifts us up where we belong." It was the memory of a cool, star-filled night in "Amazing Grace."

For me, science has been a means to the end, not an end in itself. Music, that great invisible force, has taught me that the most concrete, powerful, and transforming elements of humanity are invisible, irreducible, and immune to jargon. I think of the words of 2 Corinthians 4:18. "So we fix our eyes not on what is seen, but on what is unseen. For what is seen is temporary, but what is unseen is eternal."

The movement of the unseen into the seen, of what is felt into what is known, of what could be into what is, of the seemingly impossible into the possible, is what I call *art*. Those of us who anchor ourselves in God would also call that movement *faith*. I think of the sense of longing and hope in Rachmaninoff's *Symphony no. 2, op. 27* or in Moses' movement in faith from the riches of Egypt, through the wasteland, toward the Promised Land.

Art and faith—the transcendent touches in the routine—

provide us with the best that life has to offer, not in a continual stream of bliss, but in the waking of hope, the desire to love, and the occasional reminder that some things in life are worth pursuing. These moments, these breaks in the wall allow us to peer through to the other side: they are timeless and anchored in time; the fleeting stuff of eternity; the power of hope, joy, and love in the most hopeless situations.

The harsh juxtaposition of music with illness has produced more than its share of unexpected and gracious moments. Music, hinting at what is right and eternal, and illness, screaming at all that is wrong and given to decay: such is the breeding ground for moments of despair and hope, pain and joy, cursing or faith. Such moments have left me amazed, humbled, and drawn, more and more, to a bittersweet song.

I have only stories. In my years since taking my job as music therapist at the University Hospitals of Cleveland in 1985, I remember few specific dates and treatment plans. Only the faces and the songs stick.

When I first met Charlene, she was hooked to a huge, square box that stood next to her hospital bed. Originally diagnosed with leukemia, Charlene had successfully endured high-dose chemotherapy. Within a few months, however, she developed additional symptoms that indicated she was bleeding internally. Test after test, however, could not determine what was causing the bleeding. Charlene was wearing down under the pressure, fear, and loneliness. As I walked into her room, I noticed the pictures of her two children, whom she had not been able to see for weeks.

The huge box-like machine was designed to restore her blood count so that she could endure a bone-marrow transplant. The procedure, which can take two or more hours, requires the constant presence of a specialist who must monitor the patient's condition every fifteen minutes. When I entered the room, carrying my Omnichord, the specialist gave me a nasty look and suggested that I come back later. "I don't think this is a good time. Charlene is quite anxious and not very happy now. We've just begun the procedure." I did not make eye contact with the specialist, preferring to take my cues from Charlene. Even though she was drugged, her eyes sunk with fatigue, her long arms black and blue from repeated punctures and blood draws, Charlene was interested in the idea of music.

With much effort from a once-strong body, she lifted herself up in bed and began to strum my Omnichord. I remember we sang "Edelweiss," "You Are My Sunshine," "Amazing Grace," and the song I had written for the American Cancer Society, "We Can Cope." I told her about my battle with cancer. We connected, through music, person-to-person. At one point, I even shared a verse from Mr. Mamie's "Look on the Bright Side" song. When Charlene chuckled, the specialist said, "Maybe this was a good time, after all." The specialist even asked for a turn on the Omnichord and invited other nurses to come see. In between songs, Charlene and I talked about a host of things: her love for music, her physical discomfort, her emotional exhaustion from spending Thanksgiving in the hospital, her daughter's birthday, and the approaching Christmas holidays. She longed to be home for Christmas. "I've missed so much. I'm so tired of being here."

We talked about some ways she might use her time: listening to the radio, reading, playing instruments, composing a song. When I asked her to tell me about her children so that we could create a song for them, she began to cry. "I can't. Every time I think about them, I just cry. I just cry." The weight of her sorrow was almost palpable, like the weight in a clipped wing. Her fatigue seemed to cover everything, like the morning fog on a mountain. With Olympic spirit and every ounce of strength from her once finely tuned athletic body, Charlene had fought. She had fought so hard to get better, endured the life-sucking drugs, the endless tests, the vomiting and nausea, the circular pain, the uncertainty of diagnosis, but she continued to slip further away. She longed to be well, to be home, to be whole.

In the exhaustion, disappointment, and pain, her facial features had hardened, becoming angular, chiseled, stoic. Her hair was gone; her dignity was holding on for dear life. Yet in the music her eyes spoke of an unquenchable longing, a child-like spirit of wonder, simplicity, and unsinkable things. During one of our songs, on a day when Charlene was hooked up to this massive machine, her doctor came into her room. When I saw her surprise at the change in Charlene's countenance, I asked her if she played any instruments. She said in her best doctor's voice, "Yes. I play the accordion."

I immediately responded, "Good, I'll have an accordion in Charlene's room tomorrow so you can serenade her." Taken aback, the doctor said she would, even though it had been some time since she had practiced. Charlene and I smiled at one another. We felt a certain reversal of air in the room, from despair and fatigue to a quiet confidence and levity, from doctor to performer, patient to audience, music therapist to stage manager: a leveling of roles, a stripping of pearl-white jackets and open-ended gowns into the neutral and charged field of music, where everyone has a voice, an instrument in the outcome.

In the bowels of the hospital's basement, I found that accordion and lugged all sixty pounds of it up the elevator, down several twisted halls, and into Charlene's room. When I placed the accordian at the foot of Charlene's bed, her eyes sparkled.

The next day was a Saturday. The doctor, on her day off, came in to play the accordion for Charlene, whose family was visiting at the time. As the doctor was playing, a curious thing happened. A woman visiting her mother at the end of the hall was drawn to the music. As it turned out, this woman had been playing *her* accordion for her mother, softly so as not to disturb anyone. Well, sure enough, she was invited to join in the music, and within minutes there were dueling and jamming accordions. I mean, they let the music rip. Soon the music attracted nurses, patients, housekeeping staff, visitors, other doctors, all of them clapping hands, stomping feet, nodding heads, bopping to beat all be-bop. That was it. In the music the distinctions between roles and titles vanished. They were all just people, connected in a chain of harmony, a circle without pain or disease or intrusions, the soaring of a common and uncommon dream.

And in the motion of the dream, of the music, Charlene at last found a little strength, a little laughter, a little rest.

Music allows us to see on a higher plain. Music reminds us in some mysterious way that what we erect in the walls of our minds, those things we consider precious or pressing, are often just a whisper of another, greater reality. We get glimpses that, far from being in isolation or competition, we are connected, one with another, one with something beyond ourselves. And in those connections, I have seen other realities disappear: pain, fear, deep loss, the slow leak of need.

By its very nature, a hospital is an intrusive place: needles, diagnoses, tests, prodding fingers, electrical monitors, drugs, radiation, strange rooms, strange beds, a strange world. Relationships in a hospital are often one-way: a person becomes a *recipient* of care, of drugs, of test results, of good or bad news, in much the same way that a cow is the *recipient* of a brand. That may be overstating the issue a bit, but the movement of much of medicine is *down*: from the experts and technicians to the one who is ill.

During illness even the internal relationship—between sick people and their own bodies—often becomes skewed. When we are ill, we feel as if our bodies have somehow betrayed us, leaving us marooned in illness. Fed by isolation, fear, guilt, or a sense of powerlessness, sick people can soon begin to see themselves not just as recipients but also as victims: helpless, scared, and defeated.

Music, the gift of a song, can often restore balance, reminding people of love, beauty, laughter, touch—the correct and true movements of human relationships. At times music can transform even the most sterile and broken environment. Part of the

177

power of music, I think, is that it comes as a gift packaged to be received. Although many people often have a hard time accepting *tangible* gifts, music is disguised as another person's time, heart expression, or thoughtfulness. Music is as welcome as the face of a friend, especially when the sick person is away from home.

I think of Michael Loveman, a well-respected Jewish business-man in his mid-fifties. When I first met him, he was curled up in the fetal position, scrunched, pale, thin, and weak. His cancer was eating him alive. Yet in his pain and wasting away, he maintained a gracious spirit, a hunger for something beyond himself.

I knelt on the tile floor beside his bed so that I could talk to him at eye level. After my typical introductions, I said, "Tell me what kind of music you like, Mr. Loveman."

He spoke in a barely audible, wispy voice, with pauses of two or three seconds for breath in between words. "All kinds," he said. "Classical, orchestral." And then his voice faded.

"Vladamir Horowitz?" I asked, trying to identify with his culture. His eyes widened; he nodded slightly, seemed impressed.

"Wynton Marsalis?" he countered, asking with his voice inflection whether I was familiar with his music. I was impressed. Rarely do I meet people familiar with accomplished African-American musicians.

"Isaac Stern?" I retorted, surprising even myself with the name of a second Jewish musical artist. Get down, Deforia!

"And Kathleen Battle?" he said, realizing that he had scored a hole-in-one. With a glint in his eyes he knew he had me on the run.

I rummaged my mind for more Jewish names, and from way down deep came, "Itzhak Perlman?" I looked around to see if someone else might have given voice to this name.

Mr. Loveman smiled, hesitated. I could tell that he was

groping, searching for a name of another black musical artist. Finally pursing his lips to form another name, slowly, syllable by syllable: "Bill Cosby?"

We both laughed out loud, realizing an instant friendship, a bonding of respect.

When I returned the next day with my Omnichord, his breathing was more labored. I thought I should let him rest. "Why don't I come back tomorrow after you have had your beauty nap?"

He shook his head and spoke slowly, in measured words. "Better sing now. May not be here tomorrow." I looked him in the eyes.

"Do you think you may die?" He nodded affirmatively. "Are you ready?" I asked.

Suddenly his face took on a glow, a peace, an unmistakable strength. He nodded with assurance, the hint of a smile. Spontaneously, from I don't know where, I started to sing:

Shalom havareem, shalom havareem,
Shalom, shalom;
L'hitraot, l'hitraot,
Shalom, shalom. . .

The notes, from somewhere inside and yet somehow beyond me, were pure, sweet, haunting, ethereal. Mr. Loveman, caught up in the music, lifted an arm in the air, fluid and unstuck from pain, and began conducting the sound, the motions of longing, the connection to another reality. "Magnificent, marvelous, exquisite, gorgeous," his words came, enraptured and undisturbed. Mr. Loveman not only heard the floating notes, but he also felt a concrete connection between himself and God.

Music therapy offers techniques, training, and data-based evaluations, but it never works in a vacuum. Music, like the connection between a dying man and his God, is not something that can be reduced to the box of science. When confined to a set of rigid definitions or expectations, the music, like the caged wild bird, simply dies. The best the procedures can do is point the music in the right direction.

Patients often feel helpless, stripped of some of their humanity. The medical environment often reduces them to the role of patient, victim, the Parkinson's in 209, or the Hodgkin's on the second floor. Patients feel that they have become a financial and emotional drain on their families, the very people they most want to lift up. They long to feel human again and connected— in ways other than tube to machine—to life, community, the give and not just the take in love.

With that in mind, I must never view what I do as merely a job but as part of the complex arrangement of one person relating to another person. My job, more often than not, involves hugs or back rubs or chats as often as it does syncopation, Phrygian modes, Ravel, or Whitney Houston.

Music, in such a loose scheme, becomes the common ground. My job is simply to let music do what it does best: make connections, person-to-person, soul-to-soul, where those connections, through illness or emotional distress, have been overloaded, broken, or destroyed. In other words, in both a technical and symbolic sense, my job is to build musical bridges.

The stories of Mrs. Crary and Mrs. Clarke speak of the power and the limitations of music. Although I came to know Mrs. Crary and Mrs. Clarke at different points in my career, I see them in my mind almost as sisters. They were in so many ways alike. Both in their sixties, they were first and foremost mothers with grown children; they loved to talk about their families. Both were unpretentious women, etched with a quiet sense of dignity, almost regal. Both were cheerful, positive, Christian women touched with a sense of peace. Both loved hymns. And both longed to be free from the ravages of cancer.

Mostly they shared this: they both were deeply loved in return by their families. With each woman, I shared music, time, and stories. When I left them, I always was the one who felt blessed with an odd sense of peace—this from women whose bodies were battlegrounds. The music in each case served only to highlight their dignity, perseverance, and longing.

With both women and their families, I shared the end.

Mrs. Crary slipped into a coma. When I went to visit her in her room one day, her bed was made. Fearing the worst, I went to the intensive care unit, which was the first time on my job that I had been there. When I arrived, I didn't even recognize her; always a large woman, she had swollen to nearly twice her size. There were beeps, buzzes, urgent voices, tubes, cords everywhere. Seated next to her bed, cramped in the middle of this chaos, were Mrs. Crary's husband and son. I introduced myself, telling them how much she had talked about both of them.

When I told Mr. Crary that I would keep them in my prayers, he unexpectedly asked me to sing for her. The nurses had told me that Mrs. Crary was totally unresponsive, even to pain. I had with me the lyrics to her favorite songs; I had enlarged the words on computer paper so that she could read them with her failing sight. I laid the sheets on her chest. I placed my Omnichord near her head so that the vibrations would be close to her. Mrs. Crary's husband requested "Showers of Blessing," so I sang all the way through.

> There shall be showers of blessing, precious reviving again;
> Over the hills and the valleys, sound of the abundance of rain;
> Showers of blessing, showers of blessing we need;
> Mercy drops round us are falling, but for the showers we plead.

Next, her son asked me to sing "Down in the Valley." After that, her husband asked for "It Is No Secret What God Can Do." Even in the chaos, the noise of machines, the bark of medical command, the approaching reality of death, there was peace. Music, even here, and maybe especially here, was appropriate, soothing, connecting. Just as I was about to leave, Mrs. Crary's husband asked for one more, his wife's favorite: "How Great Thou Art." As I sang, I could see the effect the music was having on father and son; their eyes teared, and I could see in the way they held on to each word that they were saying good-bye, touching hearts one last time. As I sang the last chorus, "Then sings my soul, my Savior God to Thee: How great Thou art, how great Thou art!" we saw a twitch in Mrs. Crary's face and watched as one of her eyes popped open. I finished the song: "Then sings my soul, my Savior God to Thee: How great Thou art, how great Thou art!"

Mrs. Crary never sang, never said a word. Her husband and son, the two people dearest to her, got up from their chairs and came over to her. They exchanged no words, but they knew that, in the music, she had heard. The next day, Mrs. Crary died with both eyes closed but never for a moment blinded to the fact that she was loved.

Years later, Mrs. Clarke battled her cancer. She was a fighter. She had raised her children by herself, and when it came time to forgive, she found the courage to do that too. She would not give in to the cancer, not without one long, good, final fight. In music, she found challenge, rest, hope, and the energy to move on. I know that losing her physical strength and independence was hard. But she never sacrificed her dreams, dignity, and balance.

Her daughter, Leslie, vice-president of nursing at University Hospitals' Rainbow Babies and Children's Hospital where I work, is a friend of mine. Leslie also fought a private war. In her position and in her deep love for her mother, she could have pulled strings to get special care for her mother, but she lovingly resisted the temptation.

I enjoyed watching Leslie and her mother. It was obvious that they were friends, in love with one another. Leslie slipped in and out of her various roles—daughter, administrator, sister, nurse, mother, intercessor, transporter, and guardian—sometimes effortlessly, sometimes with much effort, but always graciously. She brought her mother flowers, pressed on Mickey

Mouse bandages with pride, drew funny faces on water jars, and even planted her a garden.

Shortly before Mrs. Clarke died, she was readmitted to the hospital. Leslie called me in tears, "Come quick, Deforia." When I got to Mrs. Clarke's room, she was shaking, jerking uncontrollably, this woman of dignity, this fighter, this mother who loved. The nurses said something about electrolytes out of balance. A song seemed so out of place, so small in the face of this tyranny, this kind of suffering. But they wanted me to sing, and I had to force something out of my mouth. I think I might have sung "Oh, What a Beautiful Morning" and "Balm in Gilead." While Mrs. Clarke shook, there was little that spoke of a new morning or a cure. I worked no magic on that particular day. I just waited, rubbing her hands, praying that the medication would take effect. In a few days she died.

I have linked the stories of Mrs. Clarke and Mrs. Crary for several reasons, not the least of which is this: the power of music, whether it spawns a miracle or seemingly nothing at all, is not so much in the excellence of song but in the connection of hearts; that connection, even in the smallest of details, results in community and dignity.

Sometimes music is the gift of transition, helping people to celebrate, grieve, say good-bye. In some cases, the music is of no direct value to the patient, but it may be of incalculable worth to a relative or a friend who has suffered, grieved, and felt loss.

I first saw Richard and Mary Beth Stirzaker in the hospital elevator. They had been pulled out of school because their mother, Maryann, was close to death. Richard was thirteen, an age of enormous transition, and Mary Beth was eight, when death is mostly something that happens to a goldfish. Both were dressed in their Catholic uniforms: Richard in dark creased slacks with a white pullover and Mary Beth in a pleated, plaid dress. They were a study in contrast. Richard was in that awkward, gangly period when boy meets man and doesn't yet recognize himself. In his eyes I sensed a mixture of confusion and wild terror. In her innocence Mary Beth was bubbly, electric in smile and eye, bouncing without a clue.

With a frightening urgency in her voice, the nurse suggested we go see their mother. Sitting in the room, beyond the glass sliding doors, was their grandfather, their mother's father. He tenderly held his daughter's hand, his head drooped. I went in first and introduced myself. He brightened, "Did you know she plays piano and is the church organist?" Always the proud father. I nodded and told him of the times his daughter and I had shared music, playing keyboards, talking about her music students and her love of the classics and hymns.

"How are things?" I asked. "I heard there was a slight improvement over yesterday."

A nurse quickly interjected, "Well, not really, her kidneys are still not working." She left no room for a false sense of hope.

Richard and Mary Beth stood outside the glass doors. I wondered what was going through their minds. Their mother tried to protect them as much as she could. She had retained her dignity through the side effects of her bone-marrow transplant. She had weathered the procession of rashes, hair loss, mouth sores, diarrhea, fevers, nausea, and vomiting. In her suffering, she worried mostly about her children.

Maryann Stirzaker wore a pink, frilly gown and a bonnet, like one from the frontier days. Even heavy with morphine, something in her eyes spoke of recognition. And then came the two of them, her children. They looked for tape to hang things on her wall: a picture of Jesus, school pictures, a small stained-glass suncatcher. Richard told his grandfather that he had found his mom's rosary, the one blessed by the pope. That was all they said. The room crackled with the awkward and nervous energy of silence and fear.

I decided to leave the two children alone with their mother. But then, no more than ten feet out the door, I turned around and said to Vickie McClure, the music-therapy intern who was following me on my rounds: "Those kids are horrified. We should try to do something for them."

Vickie and I returned to the room and asked Richard and Mary Beth if they would like to come with us and write a song for their mother. Both of them thought it was a good idea. The four of us sat down in another room with a keyboard, an Omnichord, and plenty of pencils and paper. Vickie worked with Mary Beth, and I worked with Richard, who was on the verge of tears. His facial tics, hard blinks, twitches, and worried eyes all spoke what he was unable to at the time: *I'm confused, frightened.* I asked him if he had been able to cry about his mom yet. "No," he said, before adding, "but I will." I asked him about his mother. He told me that his mom had always been his friend, his strength. He told me how he had struggled in his speech, and his mom was patient, always encouraging. He told me how she had helped him when he had trouble with his homework, and now he could do it on his own. His mom had even helped him get his arrow in Boy Scouts; she looked forward to him becoming an Eagle Scout. "If I could tell my mom something," he said, "it would be that I've gotten myself back together again. And I never could have made it without her." We talked for the next several minutes, and this is the song we finally wrote:

> I never could have made it without you.
> You taught me how to cope.
> I've gotten myself back together again.
> Because you've given me hope.
> I've learned to stand up for myself;
> You've helped me to be strong;
> My confidence and self-esteem
> Are growing right along.
> You gave me something to believe in;
> I'll try to carry on.
> Your love and affection I will sing
> It to you in a song.

Then we joined Mary Beth and Vickie. I took my seat at the piano, and Richard began to sing in a soft, soprano voice, tentatively, yet tenderly. It was beautiful. And then his sister, with the energy of a second grader performing a solo, got up and sang her song.

> It's hard to say what I want to say to you;
> You gave me a birthday cake on my birthday;
> You gave me presents for my birthday.
> We had fun on Easter; we go to church on Easter,
> I like to find the eggs.
> Grandpa and Grandma have taken good care of me.
> You made me my pants to wear and macaroni and cheese;
> It took a long time to get to the hospital.
> I love you.

We recorded both songs and then returned to the waiting room to join their dad, family, and friends. Richard and Mary Beth played the songs that we had recorded for their mother. Everyone cried.

While Richard and Mary Beth were playing their songs, I slipped into their mother's room with another copy of the tape. Their grandmother was there, keeping a vigil. I told her what the children, focusing on Richard, had done. Even before I started playing the song, she started to cry. "Richard is dyslexic and yet so musical. His mother has worked so hard with him, encouraging him, always telling him that he could do it. When others simply gave up, his mother believed in him." I played the songs. The grandmother cried, wiping back the tears to cast intermittent glances at her daughter, who didn't seem to respond. No miracles happened in Maryann Stirzaker that day, but everyone around her felt the miraculous legacy of love she had left behind.

The next morning I called Richard and Mary Beth's dad in the waiting room. I had been up during the night, thinking of the children, the family. We had some small talk about the music the children composed, and then I asked, "How is everything else?"

His words came slowly. "We will let her rest this morning." At first he fought back tears, but then he audibly sobbed. In his tears was an acknowledgment of the love shared and a loss felt. Later that same morning, Maryann Stirzaker was removed from life support. We will let her rest.

Bridges, then. Music has the power to move a person between different realities: from a broken body into a soaring spirit; from a broken heart into the connection of shared love; from death into the movement and memory of life.

And there is more. Music has the power to touch the heart of a child with God.

Angelica, six years old, tight-lipped and suspicious, had leukemia. She was mature beyond her years; she had to be. Her mother, Evelyn, was not only Angelica's mommy but also her best friend; they often conversed like two adults. When I first met Angelica, she was not easy to cajole, to steal a smile from. Sometimes I detected a you'll-have-to-work-real-hard-to-get-anything-out-of-me attitude. And I'll have to admit, I was often forced deep into my bag of tricks to get even the slightest reaction out of her. She was definitely not a kissy-huggy, teddy-bear kind of girl.

Over two years of clinical treatments, I was able to develop a solid relationship with Angelica. I brought her Bible-story coloring books and Critter County cassette tapes and visited her, sometimes even with a song, at her bedside. Her condition continued to worsen, and she grew progressively weaker. One morning, I remember, her breathing became especially labored. She asked if I would rub her chest; somehow this made her feel better. I crawled up in bed with her because she wanted me close. She protested whenever I tried to get up or even change positions. "Please don't go," she would plead, cradled next to me. "I'm scared." I asked her if I could sing a song my mother used to sing me when I was feeling sad or sick.

> Jesus loves me, this I know,
> For the Bible tells me so.
> Little ones to him belong,
> They are weak, but he is strong.

Angelica closed her eyes but was afraid to go to sleep for fear that I would leave her. I asked her, "Has anyone ever told you about Jesus?" She shrugged her shoulders. "Would you like me to tell you about him now?" She nodded. I told her that Jesus saves us from the bad things we do and that he promises us a place in heaven, where there is no pain and where the joy is beyond anything we could imagine. "He will come and live inside you," I said, "if you will just ask him to."

She prayed with me and asked Jesus into her heart. I told her that now we were sisters, with the same heavenly Father. She smiled. "We'll live in heaven together, Angelica. If you get there before I do, just remember that I'll be there soon. You'll love your home in heaven, Angelica." I kissed her and sang another verse of "Jesus Loves Me."

Shortly before Angelica was discharged from the hospital, her baby sister was to celebrate her first birthday. Angelica, who had fallen in love with her little sister, was upset that she couldn't get out to buy her a present. "What would you buy her?" I asked.

Without hesitation, she said, "A red velvet dress." I told her that I would buy a dress for her to give to her sister. That weekend, I bought two dresses: a frilly, pink dress and a red velvet dress, piped in white satin. I let Angelica decide which one she wanted to give to her sister. Angelica's eyes widened and she pointed, without a hint of doubt, to the red velvet dress. Together we composed a song, put the lyrics in a card, crayoned a border, and waited for her sister to arrive. This was to be her sister's first birthday celebration. And Angelica's last.

I attended Angelica's funeral. After sitting through the most soul-stirring rendition of "Jesus Loves Me" I had ever heard, I looked up and through my tears saw Angelica's mom. In her arms, she cradled a little girl in a red velvet dress.

Seated upon the convex mound
Of one vast kidney, Jonah prays
And sings his canticles and hymns,
Making the hollow vault resound
God's goodness and mysterious ways,
Till the great fish spouts music as he swims.

—Aldous Huxley

Chapter Eleven

The Harmony of Faith and Suffering

Melange (a blend)

Suffering hurts.

I know this is not profound; there is no hint here of abiding comfort or eternal art or easy answers. As grim as any human reality, the fact remains, sticks like fangs in the flesh of time: suffering hurts.

I wish through my own meager suffering or through entering into the experience of others' suffering that I had more to say, something to make it better: a pill, a promise, an escape, a dream of something better, a song, and a dance. I have little or nothing. In this world, suffering is sure and painful, a certain agony. We live, always, with the hint or scream of danger.

And yet I still have faith. Sometimes in the dark of a night, I'm not sure why.

I daily see the face of suffering: the father of a recent college graduate now comatose; the stab of recognition, the kindling of something in the eyes of a profoundly retarded man; a three-year-old faced with *another* needle; the way a sister, confused and enthralled, places her favorite bear at the bedside of her dead brother; the stroke of a mother's hand to comfort her son's middle-of-the-night pain. Such suffering cannot be dismissed.

Faith, if there is any power in it at all, must first recognize the reality of suffering and for a time stand amazed and silent. What is there to say, really, to a mother grieving the loss of her toddler? To a trained athlete wasting with a cancer? To a man, disconnected from his homeland, traveling another path of pain? What words are there? What thoughts, once sounded, will not simply be swallowed whole in the abyss of suffering?

I have slowly learned to respect suffering, to give it its due. Suffering is powerful: grim and dark and hideously indifferent, but nevertheless armed to the teeth. With both horror and fascination, I have watched the way people move underneath suffering, the way they rise or squirm, rise and squirm and rise and squirm, or simply call it another day. It is in the reactions to suffering, not in the force of suffering itself, that we see the central mysteries of the human spirit, the outlandish ability to carry on or break down or pray or caress a hand at the very moment when all hope seems gone.

Suffering calls out for transcendence at the same time it knocks the stuffing out of us. It asks us to accomplish the impossible, to break through gravity when we are being crushed. It should come as no surprise, then, that suffering brings out the best and worst in us. Who can predict which one of us will fall to a crippling despair or rise in a majestic grace?

I recall the faces and hands of suffering.

Kindhearted Mrs. P. had a peaceful, undisturbed face. I first met her when she came to visit her two-year-old daughter, a little redhead who had lost her hair to chemotherapy. Mrs. P. smiled, dumped out a bagful of Critter County tapes, and talked slowly, patiently, in simple, deep words. As I came to know her, she told me of her other daughter: a retarded child who had died in a nursing home. She showed me a charcoal sketch someone had drawn of her retarded daughter. In the picture the daughter, who had never walked, was dancing with Jesus. I remember her face, which should have been drawn with suffering, beaming with joy.

After her little redheaded daughter had gone home, Mrs. P. returned to the hospital at Christmas with two garbage bags full of toys. She gave the toys to one of her daughter's former roommates, whose family was destitute. Three years later, Mrs. P.'s daughter finally was well. Who can describe such patience, such simplicity of pureness, such joy?

Mr. I.'s face was lined with confusion as he looked at his son, once as bright and unfettered as the hope in his heart, now sunk in pain. The brain cancer had changed everything. His son's personality had shifted dramatically; he could no longer even hold up his head. What the parents needed was time to deal with their own grief and anger, to adjust to this little boy who, although dramatically changed, was still their own, the same child who smiled at them from a photo on a living room shelf. But time, among other things, was not available to them. The boy died quickly, virtually alone in his parents' transition. Who can know of such pressure, the hurt that presses in, buried all the way to the bones, fixed, finally, in a skeleton of remorse?

I remember the fingers of a black man, Mr. N., paralyzed from a shooting accident when he was sixteen. I remember the way those velvet fingers moved on a piano, the color that could come from eighty-eight black-and-white keys. He was smooth with me too, a picture of charm. I had been warned not to trust Mr. N., that he had a longtime drug habit, but I wanted to take a chance, to see where compassion and music might take him, to awaken in him something that had long ago died. I knew that he was going to be in the hospital a while, so I wondered if he might go from room to room and play with a hospital choir we had formed. On the keys, his fingers were magic. I left my Yamaha keyboard with Mr. N. The day before he was to be discharged, my keyboard was missing; he said his friends had stolen it. It wasn't so much that I was out $500 but the luxury of the destruction that he permitted, both of his own self and of those around him. Who can understand the depths of such depravity, the purposeful rusting of good intentions?

I remember Mrs. A.'s hands as she wiped the disfigured face of her little William, seven years old and battling a brain

193

tumor. She would stroke his forehead, wiping a tear from his eye, bathing his dry lips when he finally lay comatose. Where, in the heaviness of such hands, of such a life, did the tenderness come from? I remember Mrs. A. asking me, with a heart hungry for healing, if I worked with children in comas. She had heard things, and she was more than willing to believe.

Mr. and Mrs. P. I. N. A. They are real people, with real names, unscrambled in their PAIN, with capital letters, the megaphone of God or accident or dumb luck. Suffering, at the very least, has put them on alert, a kind of red-static burn that runs up and down the nerves.

And me, on the outside, with my song and dance. In the face of this pain I often feel so inadequate. In the faces of such suffering, what can I do with, say, a tambourine? What kind of ring do songs like "Up Where We Belong" or "Jesus Loves Me" make in the vacuum of fear? What kind of jam session do I have the right to bring to a room filled with sympathy cards? What power can a collection of notes wield against the incessant and demanding noise of pain?

There is always surprise in what I do. And it's not me so much but the bewildering endurance of such soft and fragile notions: grace, beauty, music. In them, in their very float and wonder comes the heavy stilling of mind, time, and pain. In the blare of pain's noise sounds a quiet note of longing. In the heat of panic blows a cool touch of a soul's breeze. In approaching death steals a hint of renewal. Grace, beauty, and music make cracks in the hard, impenetrable walls of suffering, not always for long, maybe just a moment or two. But in that moment is the opening for all sorts of unexpected and inexplicable realities.

Sometimes the crack leads to something quite dramatic. I think of Duane Sullivan, a man in his sixties, with a silver tongue, golden voice, and a head full of dreams. When I met Duane, he had been hospitalized for colon cancer. A former salesman for a pharmaceutical company, Duane now spent much of his time building and playing his own dulcimer. I was so impressed with Duane and his dulcimer that I bought one too and had him teach me to play it. I still remember the way the nurses, doctors, patients, and visitors would gather around when we would light into our own, mostly ad-libbed, version of "Boil Them Cabbage Down."

> Boil them cabbage down,
> Turn them hoecakes round, boys,
> Only song that I did know,
> Boil them cabbage down.

Duane, when he wasn't losing himself in music, was a man of realism and control. He never spoke much of his cancer, but I felt his fear and sadness under his placid exterior. Eventually Duane slipped into a coma, and the doctors said they could do nothing more for him. Duane's devoted companion, a beautiful and gentle blonde named Carol, refused to have his life-support system removed. Instead, she played dulcimer music by his bedside every day. For weeks Duane lay lifeless. And then, for no apparent reason, he awoke, living with much gusto for another year. Duane credited the music for punching a hole in his unconscious state. "I heard these beautiful notes," he would say afterward, "strains of music, and I had to find them. The sounds forced my mind to function as a mind should and not just sleep. They made me realize that out there was something worth looking for, something I *should* look for."

At other times, the awakenings from suffering are more subtle: a blink of an eye, a smile, an apology, a distraction from the pain, a nod of recognition. Amanda was a pixie child with a magazine-cover face: big eyes, gapped-tooth smile. Her cancer was raging; I think she knew, even in her five-year-old mind, that she would die soon. Shortly after coming to the hospital, Amanda shut down. She refused to talk to anyone, even her parents. One day as her mom talked to a surgeon who had come in the room, I went over to Amanda, took out my Omnichord, and told her that if she could tell me what song I was playing, I would leave. I played one verse, and she looked up at me with this don't-you-know-*anything* tone of voice, and said: "Old MacDonald." The doctor and mother, quite shocked, turned to look.

I continued, "And on this farm he had a . . ." and waited for a response.

"Pig," Amanda sang. Twenty verses later, the doctor finally came over and tried to talk to Amanda himself. He asked if I would follow Amanda throughout her treatment.

When she was released and then readmitted, I returned to her room with a big, colored parachute. Amanda was so weak that she could hardly lift her hand. I fastened some loops of the parachute to her IV pole and other objects in the room and gave other loops to her family members, who held up the parachute so that it formed a dome over us. As we sang and played music, I ran over to Amanda, under the parachute, and shook her hand. I pretended that her handshake was so hard that I let out a yell. Amanda, soon to die, laughed and laughed. Her family, I know, held on to the simplicity of that laugh, its color, hope, and joy. It was a life-giving memory, forever.

Cracks in the walls of suffering. My job is to look for openings for grace, hope, love, forgiveness, tenderness, beauty. The very thing that makes suffering so difficult—the immensity of its pressure—also creates the cracks, the opportunities for experiencing what might never have been possible before. Those openings may close as quickly as they open, but for at least one moment in time they provide an opportunity for change, growth, and maturity.

Suffering does not always open windows. I used to think it did, but now I know better. Suffering people often get drowned in the barrage of emotion—fear, guilt, loss, anxiety, hopelessness—or simply get stuck in the pain. Even death, with its room for one last chance, is often not experienced as a conscious, rational movement of the mind: a fact, in short, that must be dealt with. I have watched dying people never deal with the reality of death. Relationships often remain untended or broken; words remain unspoken; hopes remain unrealized. The process of dying, with its pain and fear, can so occupy a person in the struggle of the moment that past and future become distant and unimportant. Or, taken to the opposite extreme, past and future become a memory or dream of escape.

Audrey, a woman in her early fifties, had escaped with her family from Lithuania during World War II. When I met her, she was in and out of morphine, often lucid and alert, at least enough to know that she had little time left. As I talked with her, I discovered that she had a teenage son, who was distanced from her. I asked her if she would like me to write a song, hoping that the urgency of pending death would prompt her to repair her relationship with her son, or at least leave a few words for him to remember her by. "Oh, yes," she said, "I would love to write a song."

"About your family, your son?"

"No, no," she would say, "about the Baltic Sea, my beloved Baltic Sea." Even though I tried to move her thoughts to forgiveness or love, she could not stop thinking about that troubled and beautiful sea that she sailed over as a small child. Working with the bits and pieces of information that she had given me, I put together some lyrics for her. As I stood next to her bed, the music came to me on the spot. This was "Audrey's Lithuanian Dream."

> There were four of us, small children a long time ago
> on a journey far greater than we know;
> two brothers and one sister, Mom and Dad and me;
> our hearts took flight upon the Baltic Sea.
> A sea blue, of deep and purple hue;
> you sing to me a melody of waves that wash my soul,
> enfold me in your arms where there is peace without
>   alarm;
> eternally, my everflowing sea.

The Baltic Sea, the movement of peace and denial, calmed her and swallowed deeper, painful issues. The lyrics were read at her funeral; I wonder what emotions it triggered in her son.

For many people facing death, it is only the fear and pain that matters. Carol was in her late forties, childlike, with a child's love for attention. Her family were simple folk of clear faith, low key, tending to cling and stutter. Carol and I hit it off well. She had played the flute when she was younger; we

197

shared memories of music and family. I thought she was handling her situation fairly well. On the night she died, however, her nurse told me that Carol had become frightened, clutched the nurse's arm and refused to let go, literally clawing the nurse's flesh; the specter of death terrified her. Even as she gasped for her last breath, she fought a horror that overwhelmed her. The volume of this simple woman's terror shook me.

What can be said of suffering that produces in the dying moments a song about a sea, the hope of a mall, a scratching terror of the end? I could say that each suffering person is capable of making choices of faith, reconciliation, laughter, love, or forgiveness. Those who die instantly, without suffering or pain, are often denied such critical chances. But that, of course, is no real argument. Is this a world where love is the product of a spinal tap, where hope is the result of a third-degree burn, where unity springs from the pain of cancer? If it is, what does that say about God? That he simply does not exist, that he is sovereignly weak, that he is powerfully callous?

I choose to go no further.

I wish to say again, as a woman of faith, that I have no arguments about suffering. As I have said before, I do not concern myself with the *why* of suffering as much as the *where do we go from here* of suffering. I simply acknowledge suffering as a powerful and unquestionable reality, one that brings me to my knees in the hope of heaven. I respect the pain and questions of those who suffer. I trust that God is in control, even when the evidence around me is thin. And I act in whatever way I can to comfort those who suffer.

When it comes to suffering, I simply have no explanations. I say this for at least a couple of reasons. First, I do not have the mind to grasp such transcendent concepts. I understand the pain in a burn ward about as well as I could define an octave of music or the sound that a mourning dove makes. I am convinced that suffering, music, and beauty are not accidents; but they are nonetheless mysterious and beyond the reach of my tiny little mind. One of the ancient Greek philosophers once said that "the qualities of numbers exist in a musical scale [harmonia], in the heavens, and in many other things." In other words, in creation the rule is order: the mathematical exactness of laws, reason, structure, and purpose. If there is harmony in a musical scale, why should we assume, simply because we do not understand, that there is no purpose or reason for suffering?

More importantly, however, I cannot explain suffering because God does not explain suffering. When Job, a righteous man, asked God for a reason for his suffering, God "answered" him by asking Job a long series of questions: "Who marked off the dimensions of earth? What is the way to the abode of light? From whose womb comes the ice? Would you discredit my justice?"

Job finally got the point: "Surely, I spoke of things I did not understand, things too wonderful for me to know."

It seems to me that God was saying to Job, "Only when you have my wisdom, will you fully be able to understand the purpose of suffering."

Many people find little comfort here. For them, God seems to dismiss the issue of suffering in a passionless realm of superiority, refusing to act in his power to deal with the trauma of his creatures. In other words, they seem to say to God: "You seem to regard suffering with a grain of salt. Where were you when my wife was raped? Where were you when my baby died? Where were you when this or that happened to people I love?"

These same people also see Christians often dismissing suffering with a wave of the hand, the click of a tongue, or indecipherable jargon. They see Christians isolating themselves from pain and need, and confusing the need for tender mercy with a coldhearted call for judgment.

Where is the heart of God?

And the answer, of course, is this: pierced and bleeding on a hill named Golgotha, place of a skull. Although I don't understand the *why* of suffering, that does not mean that I can dismiss God as unconcerned. At the very least, the cross of Jesus Christ teaches us that God, far from being distanced from the reality of suffering, seems to embrace pain willingly. "A man of sorrows," Isaiah says of Christ, "and familiar with suffering." Jesus Christ, the God-man, weeping over Lazarus' tomb, over Jerusalem, over the effects of sin. Jesus Christ, the God-man, whipped, beaten, betrayed, mocked, rejected, spit on, crucified. The God of the Christian faith may be accused of many things, but in light of the cross of Jesus Christ, he can never be accused of apathy.

In fact, suffering, and the sin that breeds it, is a reality so great, so overpowering, so menacing, that God seemed forced to resort to desperate measures to deal with it. No magic wand, no thunderous word, no angels, no prophet, no society in the world could eliminate sin and suffering.

When God allowed humans the freedom to choose between good and evil, love and narcissism, joy and pain, and when those humans chose to sin, their choice called into existence the motion and suck of hell: a chain of grief, pain, sorrow, and suffering. God, of course, knew that would happen. He also knew that love, the purpose of creation, demanded *choice*. His dilemma, initially, was this: either to allow choice and with it the inevitable consequence of suffering, yet at the same time creating the possibility of love; or to dismiss love—real love that *chooses* to love—and be content to live without it in a world that knew no suffering. God chose in favor of love. This is messy, I know, filled with paradox and confusion, but it is, as far as I can discern, what the Bible says. I'm not sure to what extent I even know what it means.

God's next dilemma was far greater: what to do about the sin, pain, and suffering once they were unleashed into the universe? The answer, to the surprise of the cosmos, was Jesus Christ, God in human flesh. God the Father would send God the Son, clothed in human flesh, into the world to suffer and accept the consequences of sin. God himself would have to take care of human suffering. "God so loved the world that he gave his one and only Son, that whoever believes in him shall not perish but have eternal life. For God did not send his Son into the world to condemn the world, but to save the world through him."

But even after all of that, sin and pain still seem to prevail. Babies die of cancer. Puppies are hit on the road. Hitler rises to power. We yell at our children. The power of suffering is that great. So what, in the end, does the Cross really mean? What good is an escape route, really, if it does not open until the end of time? I think that the answer, in part, is that the Cross never promises to free us from pain and suffering, not at least in the present. The Cross, in fact, promises just the opposite: the certainty of pain and suffering.

But here is the mystery: the path of joy runs straight through the heart of pain and suffering. Christianity, alone among the world's religion, does not run from pain but embraces it, and then and only then does it move through it. Jesus Christ is our example of faith: "For the joy set before him endured the cross, scorning its shame, and sat down at the right hand of the throne of God." Faith, at the very least, asks us to believe this: the path to heaven runs through suffering. *Through* the sorrow of the world, *through* that certain fog of doubt and pain, we have faith: sure of what we hope for, certain of what we do not see. God is love. God is in control. God will wipe away every tear and replace it with a river of joy.

Faith carries with it movement—from what we know to what we long for, from suffering to joy, from earth to heaven. That movement, that song, is always driven and graced by the choices we make to love.

Lillian makes no special demands on life; she does not demand her rights. She is a simplistic woman, plump in her midlife years, modest in her resources. She could not quote Voltaire; she might confuse the Theory of Relativity with Murphy's Law.

Lillian has a seventeen-year-old daughter, Nashonda, who has cancer. Nashonda awaits a bone-marrow transplant; no donor has yet been found. The simple fact is this: she may die waiting. If anyone has a right to complain, to shake her fist at God, it is Lillian. But she chooses instead to love. She understands in her unassuming ways that anger, paralyzing doubt, and bitterness will only make matters worse. She needs all of her energy to care for her daughter, to cool her suffering. Yet it is more than that. Lillie believes that in the middle of the suffering, God will move her and her daughter through the pain. She believes God will provide for their needs, tenderly care for them. "It's in God's hands," she says, like a refrain. In the anchor of experience and the hope of the future, she speaks in the present tense.

But she does more than speak. She acts in love. Because Lillian does not drive, she and Nashonda take a taxi to her treatments. They have taken the trip so many times that the taxi driver has become their friend and now drives them without charge. When her daughter is in the hospital, Lillian sometimes brings evidence of Nashonda's achievements: merit roll, a good test score, her smile in a picture. She looks for ways to compliment, encourage, and give hope to her daughter, *real* ways, often small ways: a touch of her hand, a challenge in the moment, patience in her times of sorrow or hurt.

I see in this uncomplicated woman an uncommon wisdom. She has the capacity to love and not suffocate; the power to believe and not deny; the ability to find the strength, even in her doubts, in each moment's grace. When I see Lillian outside her daughter's room or drinking a cup of coffee in the cafeteria, she smiles with the gentleness born of great suffering and even greater hope.

I know that Lillian longs with all that she has to cure and comfort her daughter, to wrap her up in her chest, and to take her from the disease, the pain, the fear. She knows that she can't.

Sometimes she knows her daughter simply needs to be alone. So Lillie sips coffee, does a crossword puzzle, fixes her hair, prays. All at a distance. In her own need and fear, such a graceful and loving distance.

Bobby, severely mentally retarded since birth, had been in an institution for about two years. I met him at the hospital; he was undergoing a shunt revision, an operation to replace or unplug tubes that drain fluid from the brain.

Bobby's mom was timid and loving. I could tell by the way she interacted with him that she loved Bobby, her flesh-and-blood-and-bone.

I had seen much progress in Bobby. He was very responsive to music; he could find the sound and follow it. He could reach, grasp, hold, and shake various instruments. He was intelligent enough to be teased. "Show me the drum," I would say, "or I am going to give you the biggest kiss you have ever had." And he would laugh, a kind of all-over laugh, a shaking-face-and-body laugh. He was responsive, but without language. He could not verbalize his thoughts or feelings. But he was purposeful, capable of understanding.

In my enthusiasm, I praised Bobby's accomplishments. This made the guilt worse in Bobby's mom, who was already pinned under the distance between Bobby and her, a distance that could not be measured in the miles between her home and the institution. In moments of rare openness, she told me that her husband had given her a choice: either Bobby would leave home or he would. So there it was. She could keep Bobby at home and lose her husband, or keep her husband and lose Bobby to an institution. She loved them both.

Her husband had his reasons. He was a judge, a powerful man, who needed a home to entertain powerful people. What could he say to his guests when they entered his home and found a ten-year-old boy or, later, a teenager with diapers sitting in a wheelchair? In all fairness, she told me, her husband had tried. Then, with Bobby growing older, heavier, and less cute, the decision finally was forced on her: Which one of us do you want to leave, your son or me?

That had been two years ago, and now with me raving about her son, the guilt intensified. She knew what her son knew and didn't know. She knew when she had explained to Bobby that he was moving to a new home that he understood.

She could even see it in his eyes. She could see the distance, the soon-to-be distance between mother and child, such an unfathomable distance, the miles and miles of unceasing hurt between two hearts.

Another son to another father: "Why have you forsaken me?" Another distance, the distance between heaven and hell, was realized on the cross of Jesus Christ. Who can measure the pain in the words, who can begin to count the cost of such love? "Eloi, eloi, lama sabachthani?"—which means, "My God, my God, why have you forsaken me?"

In the divine purpose, in the plan of redemption, in the depths of love, in the agony of faith, in the certainty of final victory, and through the cross thunders this reality: suffering hurts.

God knows, suffering hurts.

Music is God's best gift to man;
The only art of heaven given to earth,
The only art of earth we take to heaven.

—Walter Savage Lander

Chapter Twelve

The Magic of the Moment

Coda (a supplement)

*I*n the dark, shades pulled, her head nearly covered with sheets, Beth Bradstock lay in the hospital bed. At the age of seventeen, once a picture of beauty, Beth was hooked like a marionette to four IV tubes, just a few of the many connections to a life gone haywire. A rare blood disorder had left her hospitalized for several months, on the edge of death.

When the child-life staff of the Rainbow Babies and Children's Hospital requested my services, they added, "Don't expect much. She probably won't speak to you, let alone participate in music. Do what you can. She has simply shut down."

There she was, in that far corner. Alone. I took a deep breath, fired a prayer along my nerves, and walked into her room. "Hi, Beth. My name is Deforia, and I'm here because I hope that music might help you with the boredom while you're at the hospital, and I was wondering if you might answer one question before I left." "I Have a Dream" this speech was not. The words were awkward and self-protective, offered up on a jet stream of concern: I did not want to intrude on a life already filled with unimaginable pain. I stood nervously, waiting for her response.

I might have winced, waiting for her reply. I summoned

the courage to look into her eyes. She nodded a yes. I was stunned by the beauty in those eyes, beauty that the disease simply could not touch. "Beth, what would you tell another hospitalized teenager who has to face something like you are facing?" She was still dazed, having just awakened, and the tubes made it difficult to swallow or talk, but she said, "Just don't give up." On a yellow tablet, I wrote down the words. I told her she seemed very wise and asked her what had given her this idea. She said, "Mom." Her mom had been there for her when she needed her the most. It wasn't so much what her mom *did*—saying the right things or taking away her pain or making her promises—but simply her *presence* that meant so much to her. Beth knew she was loved, precious. She wanted to let her mom know, whatever the future might hold, that she loved her, and to keep on. I asked her if she would mind if we set her idea to music. She said, "Okay," smiling weakly.

To each of us is given only a moment. Each moment.

Our faith, while uniquely and powerfully tied to past and future, is all about *now*: What will I do, in this moment of time, to reflect God's love and grow in Christ? I don't mean to make this sound unnecessarily complex or simplistically naïve. For if my life has taught me anything up to this point, it is that God does not want me to fall into the equally paralyzing mind-set that allows us to be preoccupied with theory or ignorant of reality. I must not succumb either to being overwhelmed by the weight of things or, in the other extreme, to having a faith so light as to be without gravity. In either case, faith must take the form of action, grounded forever in the moment.

And each moment is potential magic. Crippled by the limitation of language, I must return to the metaphor of music. In a carefully and gracefully orchestrated song, each moment of each movement is critical to the power of the music. The song may have many notes—high, low, dissonant, supporting, sudden, overpowering, innocuous, harmonic, repetitive, oppositional, even silent. But when the music is sublime, there are simply no unimportant notes.

Each day offers us a song. Each moment is important, vital, pregnant with possibility. I have come to mean this. One of the great blessings of my battle with cancer has been the value that I now place on time: the movements in each day, each hour, each minute; I find it much more difficult to take them for granted or to squander such a precious commodity on gossip, envy, or idleness. This, too, is a gift: "Teach us, Lord, to number our days aright, yes, establish the work of our hands." For the song ends.

I don't mean to sound overly dramatic. Each moment is not, and should not be, a fireworks display, a climax of color and emotion. We all know better than that. If each note in a song were a crescendo or a climax or a high C, the music would be intolerably chaotic, frenetically overbearing. Life and song are this: excitement, joy, and rapture balanced with repetition, longing, and strife. Yet even the sour notes of life—the lostness in dissonance, the loneliness in silence, the pain in failure—are not without purpose and are never completely immune to redemption, grace, and a certain magic.

I have come to love the verses in Ephesians 5:15–20:

> Be very careful, then, how you live—not as unwise but as wise, making the most of every opportunity, because the days are evil. Therefore do not be foolish, but understand what the Lord's will is. Do not get drunk on wine, which leads to debauchery. Instead, be filled with the Spirit. Speak to one another with psalms, hymns and spiritual songs. Sing and make music in your heart to the Lord, always giving thanks to God the Father for everything, in the name of the Lord Jesus Christ.

For Christians, each moment is an opportunity. Each action carries an eternal consequence. We should not be in a drunken stupor about this. We must be wise, filled with the Spirit, knowing God's will. One Bible translation says our purpose is to "redeem the time."

This is heavy stuff, carrying the load of eternity in every moment. Yet just when the weight seems a bit too much, the verses shift dramatically: from the level and vulnerable plain of caution, evil, and sobriety to the soaring and effervescent wings of music. This is what I like to think the passage says: in each moment, evil and heavy as it may be, is the potential for the outbreak of a song. Such are the notes of redemption.

Together, Beth and I composed in the dark. I asked her to pick a rhythm on my Omnichord; she sat up and picked a slow rock sound. I started to sing some lyrics, "Just don't give up. Just don't give up. If you let your hopes go down, it will be harder to. . . ."

I paused, and she picked up ". . . to get around." For the next forty-five minutes, we composed her song; near the end, buzzers and beepers sounded because she was moving, breathing deeper. The nurses scurried around us, but Beth never looked away, focusing all of her attention on the song. Then we finished a second stanza:

> Just don't give up.
> Just don't give up.
> It's not always just your words of cheer,
> But you have helped me just by being here.
> Just don't give up.

I asked her what she thought. She wanted to sing it with me. Beth—a fatal disease in her blood, with countless tubes in her wasted body, without a hope for a future—sang. Sweetly, over and over. I knew that she was tired, yet refreshed. She slept quickly. I left the yellow sheet of paper, our scribbled lyrics. *Just don't give up.*

We must have some boundaries. Although I never wish to be limited by a job description, I must for the sake of my sanity, if nothing else, erect some fences indicating how far I am capable of going. My fences are

Don't ask the *why* question.

Don't bang your head on what you are incapable of doing.

Don't pump your ego on what you are capable of doing.

Babies with cancer, little girls with a leg severed at the knee, abusive parents, the way death often swallows up the last ounce of energy and hope, the look in a mother's eyes on the day of her child's last, weak grasp—these things are beyond me. I simply choose to believe, by an act of will and by the authority of the Word of God, that God, somehow, is in control. My sanity demands that must be enough. In the end, whether I know the *why* of things does not change the *what* of things.

My greater struggle, I think, is feeling that I should be doing more. Sometimes with my bags of kazoos and maracas, I feel so helpless, so limited in the face of such suffering. I feel like a match in a desert night. Although I know of music's inherent and transcending powers, I am often frustrated, even when the wall cracks a bit. What does it mean, in the light of eternity, for a person to experience a last taste of dignity or beauty or inner healing? Of what real and lasting value is that? Again and again, I have to remind myself that I am simply to do what God leads me to do and leave the question of eternity with him.

My greatest struggle, though, probably lies in the opposite error: taking pride in what I *am* capable of doing. The awards, recognition, requests for speaking engagements, credentials, certificates, and publicity have not helped. I have become more uncomfortable with praise for fear of "thinking more highly of myself than I ought." The limelight, if it does nothing else, can blind me to the fact that I am, in a real sense, not my own. When pride sets in, it is easy for me to begin to believe that I am in control of my own time. I begin to believe that moments are mine to do with what I please.

It is then that I need to remind myself that time is a gift, not a possession. For in the passing of every second and every note, God's grace is always present. Pride or negligence creeps into our lives when we begin to draw lines of distinction that, in the end, are not really there. It is easy to break down time into what belongs to me and what belongs to him. I, for example, have often struggled with my "achievements" and "failures." Although I often say that God gets the glory, I sometimes find myself taking credit for my success and recognition. Isn't it true that I have spent hours and hours praying, studying, thinking, searching, and disciplining myself to perform better? And isn't it true that I have been given the awards, plaques, certificates, responses, and credentials to prove that? At the same time I know that God's grace has been imprinted, time and again, on my life.

I often feel guilty over sin, over blessings. *But, Lord, I don't deserve this!* I don't feel I have done anything special or extraordinary. Extraordinary is this: the widow, unobserved except by Christ, who gives her last two coins. The mother, in the dark of a room of a now-dead son, who chooses to keep believing, to keep pursuing any trace of light. The Sunday school teacher, unseen and unappreciated by most, who faithfully teaches, loves, week after week after week.

I think of the heroes in my life. They are, in the eyes of the world, nobody great. They have not built skyscrapers or won Oscars or bathed themselves in the limelight. The gifts that God has given them, they see not as tools to draw attention to themselves, but rather as a way of enriching the lives of others and bringing glory to God.

I think of those heroes in my life, at the same time common and uncommon: David Conner, the organist at the church I grew up in as a child, still there to this day, who can play anything at anytime; Mrs. Ruby Springer, youth council director in my teenage years and now a Sunday school teacher, whose example and worth are far above rubies; Mrs. Thelma Wentworth, now eighty-five, who loves with a pure heart and continues to serve the Lord with her daily prayers and praise; Bishop Marshall Gilmore, my pastor during my teenage and college years, who masterfully blended intelligence, style, and love; and pastors Robert Ferguson, a short man who stands tall and bold in God's grace, and Eddie Hawkins, who sees everything, says what is necessary, and laughs like he means it.

And my greatest hero—tireless, but sometimes worn down; patient, but sometimes feeling the pinch; faithful, but sometimes doubting why evil often seems rewarded; steady, but sometimes shaken; loving, kind, the man who most clearly shows me the unconditional love of the Father; earnest, always Ernest.

When these, my heroes, have struggled so much, often working diligently without reward or recognition, why have I been so richly blessed for doing far less? What have I done to deserve such attention? Yet, I am learning to relax, to graciously accept God's blessings, to balance a sense of responsibility with a penetrating joy, to make the most of every opportunity and, at the same time, realize that I will sometimes fail. I have slowly come to realize that I should view my life, the collection of those individual moments, as totally his. I must resist the temptation to erect the false distinctions of *my part* and *his part*.

In each moment in the song that is life, both the composer and the musician are present. When grace is at work, there is only a oneness, a unity of soul, a losing of the parts into the whole. Such is the real magic of the moment.

Just don't give up.
Just don't give up.
It's not always just your words of cheer,
But you have helped me just by being here.
Just don't give up.

After Beth Bradstock's funeral, her mother found a crinkled, yellow sheet of paper in Beth's suitcase. It was a scribbled poem entitled, "Just Don't Give Up." She wondered where these lyrics came from, who wrote them.

A week after the funeral, I sent Beth's mother a letter. I told her about the times that Beth and I had together. I wanted to let her know how much Beth loved her and talked about her. I told her that despite the many IV tubes that were hooked up to Beth, despite the distracting beep and whir of machines, despite the interruption of the nurses, Beth had focused her waning energy to compose a song. I then wrote the lyrics to the song that Beth had written.

The day after Beth's mother received the letter, she called me, crying. She had always wondered about that crumpled, yellow sheet of paper. Those words had been a source of great encouragement. She went on to tell me that she and Beth had been inseparable, best friends. And now she knew: Beth had written those lyrics for her. *Just don't give up.*

The magic in each moment is different. This goes without saying, I think, but I'll say it anyway: no one knows what will happen next. In my job as music therapist, it may be something dramatic like a woman who awakens from a coma or a dying husband who sings one final time the song that he sang to his wife when they dated. But probably not. Usually the magic is more mundane than that, a lot like life, but in some cases no less moving: a turn of a head, a touch of a hand, a blink of recognition, or a half-smile from someone who is losing heart.

The tool that I use, music, is powerful indeed. Who can understand the way it moves in the head, the heart, or someone's soul? What memories does it stir: the ocean spray in a child's cheek, the sun's angle on a distant and loved face, the cut of spring into that one long winter, a tone in the firstborn's flesh? And who can explain the weight of the emotions that are carried on a song: grief, hope, joy, love, sorrow, maybe just one, maybe one and another, maybe all the bittersweet stirrings of what it means to be alive? I can't say with any certainty.

But I do know that music has the unique power to do what often seems impossible: to open us precisely where we had shut down; to touch us where nothing had ever moved; to heal us with a blood-red chorus in an approaching dusk; to sear us with a beauty or a longing that runs up and down the spine. This, for me, is certain: music is a window where once was only a solid wall. Music is a window of opportunity, discovery, art, grace, a seamless break in the picture of any world that might have gone wrong.

As highly as I think of music and its powers to dissect, change, and heal, I am often tempted to downplay its role in what I do as a music therapist. Other elements are also at work. They also are intangible, beyond quantification, never at rest on the very razor edge of what cannot be explained. Yet they are defined to us in simple, monosyllabic words: faith, love, touch.

Much of my work extends beyond the boundaries of my job description. I do not just apply music to help treat physiological and psychological aspects of an illness or disability. I could never, as an ambassador of Christ, be so callous or calculating. Sometimes I don't play music at all; I just talk to a patient, encourage, listen, suggest a hope, allow a person to dump the fear or anger. Sometimes I stroke a hand. Sometimes I am courageous enough to do nothing at all; an acknowledgment of suffering should, at critical times, command a helpless respect for the emptiness.

For me, it often comes down to this: What can I do in this moment to develop the presence of Jesus Christ *in* me and *for* others? During those dark and seemingly God-silent days of suffering with cancer, I finally came to realize that my questions, no matter how sincere or anguished, prompted no real answers. My demand for systematic theology, like Job's, was blown away in the whirlwind that is God. I learned—slowly, painfully, and finally with a mysterious joy—that God's only sure answer was his presence. That was, after all, the reason for his incarnation: to know what it was like, in the flesh, to be *with* us. Immanuel. To suffer, even, so that he might be able to comfort those who suffer.

Christ asks nothing more from us than what he has already done himself. As I see those who suffer, I try to remember those overwhelming verses in Matthew: "For I was hungry and you gave me something to eat, I was thirsty and you gave me something to drink, I was a stranger and you invited me in, I needed clothes and you clothed me, I was sick and you looked after me, I was in prison and you came to visit me."

Through the power of Christ, in my expression of his presence to others, I comfort the One who has suffered for us. With each moment comes the possibility of entertaining an angel unaware. Or, even beyond that, Jesus Christ himself.

Music as Medicine
is also available in a video presentation.